Making Country Rustic Wood Projects

Patrick Spielman

 Sterling Publishing Co., Inc.   New York

Library of Congress Cataloging-in-Publication Data

Spielman, Patrick E.
   [Making country-rustic furniture]
   Making country rustic wood projects : original designs from
Spielman's Wood Works / Patrick Spielman ; drawings by Mark
Obernberger.
       p.   cm.
   Previously published as: Making country-rustic furniture. c1985

   ISBN 0-8069-7258-0 paper

   1. Furniture making.   2. Country Furniture.   I. Title.
TT194.S65   1990 ˏ
684.1′042—dc20

1   3   5   7   9   10   8   6   4   2

© 1985 by Patrick Spielman
Published by Sterling Publishing Company, Inc.
387 Park Avenue South, New York, N.Y. 10016
Originally published under the title
Making Country-Rustic Furniture
Distributed in Canada by Sterling Publishing
℅ Canadian Manda Group, P.O. Box 920, Station U
Toronto, Ontario, Canada M8Z 5P9
Distributed in Great Britain and Europe by Cassell PLC
Artillery House, Artillery Row, London SW1P 1RT, England
Distributed in Australia by Capricorn Ltd.
P.O. Box 665, Lane Cove, NSW 2066
Manufactured in the United States of America

Table of Contents

Acknowledgments

I am especially grateful to each member of the Spielmans Wood Works' "family." Their dedication to excellence is indeed inspiring, contagious, and well reflected within these covers. A special thank-you goes to my son and General Manager Bob Spielman for his constructive, practical, and innovative ideas. Many thanks to our chief draftsman and expert craftsman Mark Obernberger. These two people did the hard work in the trenches of our business, leaving me unencumbered to prepare this book. Much love and gratitude goes to Mrs. Pat (our overseer) and to our daughter Sandy. Their special consideration during the final, hectic days of this work is indeed cherished. A hearty thank-you to Julie Kaczmarek for the perfect typing.

Finally, and with much gratitude, I would like to acknowledge our customers and woodworking friends. Without their encouragement, efforts of this sort would not be as much fun. Thank you all!

Introduction

Over the years, the public and woodworkers alike apparently have become convinced that quality woodwork can only be made from the very best grades of perfectly dried materials. Furthermore, it has been assumed that every surface must be sanded extremely smooth and finished faultlessly. Until now, we have probably lacked the courage or inclination to question these "established principles," much less to devise some different ideas.

Today, however, a growing number of woodworkers is desperately searching for viable alternatives to conventional woodworking practices (Illus. 1). Woodcrafters are looking for inexpensive, practical materials, easy-to-master construction techniques, and simple, but professionally designed projects, developed especially for low-grade wood (Illus. 2–3). One of the reasons many woodworkers now choose green wood for their projects (Illus. 4) is because of the techniques outlined in my book *Working Green Wood with PEG* (Sterling Publishing Co., 1980). Woodworkers simply need economical raw materials. The exorbitant prices and scarcity of lumber are evident everywhere, especially for select grades of hardwoods. The costs of

Illus. 1. Many furniture makers are looking for ways to incorporate the "natural look" into their designs. For this table top, craftsman Bob Spielman has used the natural lines, or wayne edges, from the tree.

Illus. 2. A popular trestle bench made of log-run, rough-sawn cedar.

Illus. 3. Another popular Spielman design is this sturdy and comfortable park bench.

Illus. 4. A candle holder made from a disc that has been treated with PEG, which prevents cracking and keeps the bark intact. This process is also suitable for large furniture.

logging, sawing, drying, storing, and shipping have increased substantially in recent years.

When attempting to use a low-grade or other economical material to make fine furniture according to conventional construction techniques, we are certain to encounter all sorts of familiar problems. What we need are plans and designs made especially for low-grade, economical materials (Illus. 2–3).

This book represents a major effort at Spielmans Wood Works (Illus. 5) to develop a series of fundamental construction techniques that can be easily mastered and applied to make a wide variety of projects. The results (Illus. 6–7) have a specific look that is both durable and serviceable. Most of our designs are a combination of the traditional country and the rough-and-rugged rustic styles. Thus evolved the term country-rustic.

Our designs are probably more appropriate to rural than urban environments. Our design objective is to make wooden furniture that is (1) functional (comfortable), (2) durable, (3) massive in appearance and strong, but that remains pleasing to the eye, (4) constructed of economical materials, and (5) capable of being constructed easily by amateurs and advanced craftsmen employing construction techniques that are uncommonly fast, easy, and sound.

Some projects are made from logs, fence posts (Illus. 8), and used or otherwise wasted boards and planks. Most of the pieces illustrated in this book are made from unsurfaced rough-sawn boards and planks in low-grade softwood.

In most rural areas of the country you can find someone who operates a small lumber mill and who will sell you small quantities direct. Rather than cut out natural defects, like knots and wormholes, sap streaks, mineral stains, and bark edges, make them a focal point or a specific feature of a project (Illus. 9–11). Even some splits and

Illus. 5. Spielmans Wood Works, a family-operated retail business and gift shop, is located in Fish Creek, Wisconsin. In addition to their own products, Spielmans also sells crafts made by other woodworkers.

Illus. 6. This unusual table-and-bench-set design is the result of the combined efforts of several people at Spielmans Wood Works. See page 159 for plans. Most such plank-type designs include room for materials to expand and shrink.

Illus. 7. Other original designs include swing sets, which are said by many to be the most comfortable, most durable, and most functional swings they have ever seen. (Copyright by Spielmans Wood Works.)

Illus. 8. Inexpensive fence posts, like this one, are sawed lengthwise as a first step in making tapered shingles. (See page 74.)

Illus. 9. This turned lamp base, in wormy butternut with a large knothole, certainly captures the natural qualities of the wood.

Illus. 10. An antique carving in wormy wood.

Illus. 11. This practically useless knot-filled pine slab makes a beautiful clock. All surfaces were conventionally sanded and finished.

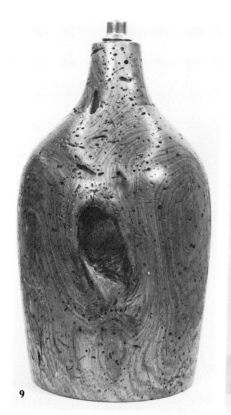

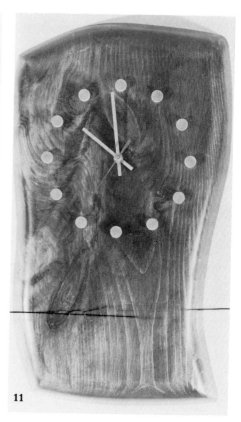

checks are acceptable in the finished product if they are not physically dangerous and if they do not weaken the structure. If the natural qualities are emphasized as much as possible, you'll be amazed at how people will appreciate this style of furniture.

Most softwoods are more interesting and, in fact, more attractive with raw, rough-sawn surfaces (Illus. 12) than they are with smooth, sanded surfaces. We give the rough-sawn surfaces just a little, but sufficient, "touch sanding" to free them from dangerous slivers while maintaining their rustic appeal (Illus. 13).

Why should craftsmen attempt to hide knife, rasp, or saw-teeth marks? What's wrong with a knot or a knothole? Why must we always finish the wood? Have you ever seen aged, unfinished, beautiful antique pine furniture? It's a look that cannot be imitated with any kind of finish. Have you ever seen rough-sawn boards (smooth ones too) that have been left unfinished and exposed to the weather (Illus. 14)? The elements turn the wood a silver grey that's very pretty indoors or outdoors. So, we may want to question some of the long-held reasons for always applying a layer of synthetic plastic or varnish that produces a less-than-natural look.

Many woodworkers and manufacturers give their products that perfectly executed, spit-and-polish finish. They seem almost too well made; the woods are exactly matched, perfectly sanded and maybe a bit monotonous. Such fine workmanship might resemble that of an imitation piece in which the grain, texture and patterns are perfectly copied in plastic laminate or vinyl veneer.

Maybe we should finish or paint an object only if it improves its function. I have included in chapter 4 some general information on finishing. At Spielmans Wood Works we make every effort to avoid excessive sanding and complex finishing whenever possible. Sanding and finishing are, in fact, dirty, tedious, difficult, and uninteresting

Illus. 12. The smooth, routed edges around these numbers make an interesting contrast with the rough-sawn wood from which they were cut. Refer to Making Wood Signs (Sterling Publishing Co., 1981) for more sign-making ideas with rustic materials.

Illus. 13. This trestle table-and-bench set, with touch-sanded, rough-sawn rustic surfaces, makes an attractive addition to an outdoor area. (Copyright Spielmans Wood Works.)

Illus. 14. A closeup look at the Spielman bench back with the country heart design. Although the surfaces look roughly textured, they are actually quite smooth to the touch. (Copyright by Spielmans Wood Works.)

anyway, so why not save time and avoid the drudgeries when you can? Most of the projects illustrated in this book require no more than ten minutes of power sanding (Illus. 14) and much less time in hand sanding. We hand-sand just to remove pencil marks, splinters, or the feathering that is produced after sawing or routing. Tooth and knife marks are not removed, since they are the visible features, or signatures, of man on his work, just as the knots, checks, and wormholes are signatures of nature.

People certainly like our country-rustic furnishings and products. Perhaps they are tired of the spit-and-polish finish of fine furniture, which old-school, conventional woodworkers might find hard to believe. However, many woodworkers have seen our designs and finished works and have recognized this trend. More and more of them have kindly asked to purchase our plans and learn the essentials of our construction techniques (Illus. 15). This book was written in response to that growing interest. Most of the designs illustrated herein are original ideas and developments of Spielmans Wood Works. They are the sole property of Patrick Spielman or Spielmans Wood Works and are copyrighted as such. Many of our designs and plans were previously prepared for sale and subsequently copyrighted, registered with the U.S. Patent and Trademark Office, and sold by us and through various dealers before we were asked to put this book together. We certainly have no objection to anyone using plans they have purchased or plans contained in this book to make projects for their own use. However, *we retain all rights to our designs and prohibit the use of our plans and designs for production and resale in any form without prior written permission from the author* (Illus. 16).

To order plans by mail, see the list on page 159. Most of these items can also be ordered from us in premachined, ready-to-be-assembled kits.

Illus. 15. Many of the author's designs feature construction details with plugs and pegs, like those shown here, which add to the rustic effect. (See page 58.)

Illus. 16. To discourage commercial imitations, a special brand is burned into all Spielmans' assembled products and kits.

Metric Equivalency Chart

MM—MILLIMETRES   CM—CENTIMETRES

Inches to millimetres and centimetres

INCHES	MM	CM	INCHES	CM	INCHES	CM
⅛	3	0.3	9	22.9	30	76.2
¼	6	0.6	10	25.4	31	78.7
⅜	10	1.0	11	27.9	32	81.3
½	13	1.3	12	30.5	33	83.8
⅝	16	1.6	13	33.0	34	86.4
¾	19	1.9	14	35.6	35	88.9
⅞	22	2.2	15	38.1	36	91.4
1	25	2.5	16	40.6	37	94.0
1¼	32	3.2	17	43.2	38	96.5
1½	38	3.8	18	45.7	39	99.1
1¾	44	4.4	19	48.3	40	101.6
2	51	5.1	20	50.8	41	104.1
2½	64	6.4	21	53.3	42	106.7
3	76	7.6	22	55.9	43	109.2
3½	89	8.9	23	58.4	44	111.8
4	102	10.2	24	61.0	45	114.3
4½	114	11.4	25	63.5	46	116.8
5	127	12.7	26	66.0	47	119.4
6	152	15.2	27	68.6	48	121.9
7	178	17.8	28	71.1	49	124.5
8	203	20.3	29	73.7	50	127.0

12 inches = 1 foot

3 feet = 1 yard

$(°F - 32) \times 5/9 = °C$

1 Wood Materials

Obtaining wood for making country-rustic objects is far more economical and much easier than obtaining material for conventional woodworking objects (Illus. 17–19). Once you recognize the potential for discarded or low-grade materials (Illus. 19), you will start to notice nearby sources for these kinds of wood. The first requirement of the material is always dictated by how or where it is to be used—indoors or outdoors. Secondary considerations include appearance, availability, service, and cost.

17

18

19

Illus. 17. Don Jackson carved this beautiful weed pot from a weatherworn, 100-year-old fence post. Note the contrast between the rough, cracked texturing and the smooth, sanded, and finished surface.

Illus. 18. Low-grade construction materials were used to make this coffee table. Extra thickness was achieved by gluing a layer of 1-inch (¾-inch) planks to heavier 2-inch (1½-inch) planks.

Illus. 19. Rough-sawn 2 × 4's and split cedar posts were combined to make this unusual planter.

HARDWOODS VERSUS SOFTWOODS

Woods with the least tendency to swell and shrink are the easiest to work with and will produce the best results. Hardwoods, which are heavier and denser than softwoods, are much more susceptible to humidity and temperature variations and thus to distortions. Consequently, the dense hardwoods are much less suitable for exterior use. And, unless commercially kiln-dried by professionals with expensive facilities, hardwoods also perform poorly in heated interiors. Softwoods, on the other hand, are more easily conditioned for indoor use. Furthermore, if products are designed specifically to allow for expansion and contraction of various components, fewer problems will arise than if assembled according to conventional designs. The advantages of softwoods include:

1. Softwoods are more easily and quickly dried.
2. They are more stable and tend to warp less.
3. They are easier to work—lighter in weight, easier to handle, easier to machine, and easier to fasten together.
4. Softwoods are generally less expensive than comparable hardwoods.
5. They are more abundant.
6. In lower grades, softwoods are excellent alternatives for many interior projects (Illus. 18).
7. Some softwood species weather better, with less checking and decay.

Some softwoods have properties essential to both indoor and outdoor products. Woods with many such characteristics are the cedars (Illus. 20 and 21), Eastern and Western white pine, sugar pine, cypress, and redwood. Of the cedars, Western red is probably one of the most available species for woodworkers (Illus. 21). Northern white and Western red cedar, cypress, and redwood are more resistant to decay than other species. Western hemlock, ponderosa pine, the spruces, and yellow poplar are also good; fir, larch, and Southern pine are slightly inferior in quality. Your native woods may be the most economical of all. Check around. Local sawmills may offer rough-sawn material, which is always cheaper than smooth or surfaced boards (Illus. 22).

SAWING OF BOARDS

How a board or plank is cut from a log affects its resistance to warping. Boards are cut from logs in two basic ways: plain-sawed and quar-

Illus. 20. 1-inch-thick and 2-inch-thick rough-sawn white cedar boards.

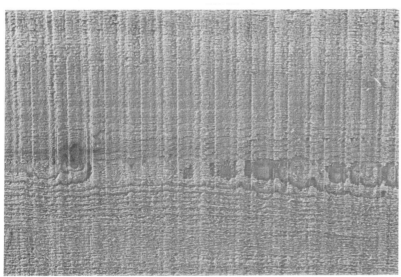

Illus. 21. Exterior grade Western red cedar with rough band-sawn texturing, as purchased from a lumberyard.

Illus. 22. Rough circular-sawn planks have a more interesting surface texture than do the same planks with smooth surfaces.

tersawed (Illus. 23). Quartersawed boards (both hardwoods and softwoods) shrink much less in drying than do plain-sawed ones. They also warp much less. Plain-grain hardwood boards are prone to curl, or "cup" (Illus. 24–25). Also, wide boards are more prone to cup than narrow ones. In general, avoid using a board wider than eight times its thickness, the point where excessive cupping could become a serious problem. A 1 × 8 is pushing the limit; a 1 × 10 exceeds it. Narrow pieces glued together to make a larger panel are less prone to cup than one solid board of the same width (Illus. 26). Wood performs better outdoors when placed in the furniture bark side out. For example, in a picnic table or bench seat, the bark side of all boards should be up.

Illus. 23. Boards cut from a log. (Left) Quartersawed (vertical grain) and (right) plain-sawed (flat grain). Quartersawed boards swell and shrink across their width only half as much as plain-sawed boards.

Illus. 24. Drying distortion, such as cupping in this plain-sawed oak, is usually more evident in dense hardwoods than in softwoods.

Illus. 25. This plain-sawed cedar shows little cupping. For most projects the bark side, which weathers best, should be placed face up.

Illus. 26. A typical rough-sawn panel made by edge-gluing four narrow boards together. This was followed by touch sanding, which creates this rustic, textured effect.

BUYING NEW SOFTWOOD LUMBER

All softwoods are commercially graded into two distinct categories: (1) construction lumber, which is used for buildings and (2) remanufacture lumber, which is used for mouldings, cabinets, and so on. The lower grades from both groups are suitable for making country-rustic projects (Illus. 27–29). Understanding all of the ratings and the various value systems for grading softwood boards and planks is very difficult. Within each of the major categories are numerous subdivisions that are broken down yet again. The easiest approach is to consult your building products dealer.

In general, avoid buying softwoods that are graded highly; they have names such as select, prime, clear, and all heart. The more practical and economical grades are called common (Nos. 1, 2, 3, and 4) and factory, or shop, grades (Nos. 1, 2, 3, and 4).

Illus. 27. Typical board quality in a utility grade, which is ideal for making many country-rustic projects.

Illus. 28. Boards in the construction grade are also economical.

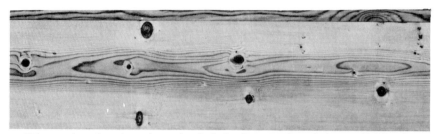

Dimension lumber (nominal 2 inches and up) is available from most lumberyards in construction or utility grades in pine, hemlock, or spruce. This material is also appropriate for many of the projects in this book.

Local mills may grade their cuttings according to their own system, which may be simplified into the following categories: clear, knotty, seconds, and rejects. Other mills may have only one grade, called log run, which includes good and bad boards. Yet another may offer "sound and better." This doesn't have any so-called seconds or rejects, and it may or may not have clear or select boards.

In dealing with commercial lumberyards or individual sawmills, always ask what grades are available, their prices, and also be sure to look over the material before buying it. Sometimes the dealer will let you pick out only those pieces that you want, if you offer to pay somewhat more than the asking price.

All of the lower grades of softwood are naturally the most economical. They are often not kiln-dried, and they contain knots and other imperfections, such as wormholes, pitch pockets, shake stains and splits (Illus. 30). These grades are sometimes available unsurfaced. This material will impart to your work a certain beauty that is rustic and natural-looking. Your success depends a great deal on your ability to match the type of wood to the required characteristics of the proposed project. For example, pine is not suitable for the legs of a picnic table. The surfaces that contact the soil will decay unless the wood is treated with a suitable preservative. Refer to page 84 for information about sealers and preservatives. Rather than treat wood with preservatives, select the correct wood for your specific application.

Illus. 29. For projects that require extra thickness, use regular 2 × 4's and 2 × 6's, which are available from your building products supply center.

Illus. 30. Wormy and rough-sawn woods with knots add visual interest to common projects.

PRESSURE-TREATED WOOD

Wood that has been pressure-treated is ideally suited to the outdoor projects, particularly those that touch the ground, including planters, patio and garden furniture, patios and wood walks (Illus. 222). Pressure-treated lumber is often an ideal alternative to the more expensive grades of redwoods and cedars. It is guaranteed to last more than 50 years if manufactured with appropriate chemicals.

Species of pressure-treated wood include the low-cost and plentiful Southern pine, ponderosa pine, hemlock, and Douglas fir. Various construction grades are available. Check for the best buy that will fulfil your design requirements. Pressure-treated wood is usually recognizable by a light green color, which is the result of chemical processing in a steel chamber at 180 pounds per square inch (p.s.i.). If left unstained or unpainted and exposed to the weather, pressure-treated wood will age to a beautiful silver grey. Just like other construction or utility boards and lumber, pressure-treated wood is usually available only smooth or surfaced (Illus. 29). Should you prefer a rustic, rough-sawn surface, however, you can skin-cut any board or lumber having smooth surfaces with a band saw to achieve a rough-cut look. Refer to page 35 for more information about this technique.

LOCAL SAWMILLS

These small mills are appearing in many communities all over the United States. They are essentially rural, one-man operations that service their own and neighboring wood lots (Illus. 31). Check your Yellow Pages for listings; you may be surprised at the services and various materials they offer. A local mill has a lot to offer. In addition to having the potential to custom-saw to your specifications, they are a good source for seconds and rejects. This is the material most other

Illus. 31. Local sawmills are a great source for inexpensive rough-sawn wood and for good slabs or log edgings. Often the mill will cut to your specifications.

Illus. 32. Perfect for rustic projects, these typical slabs are often just thrown away or sold for firewood.

woodworkers discard. Slabs (Illus. 32) and lumber that is knotty, wormy, stained, wayne-edged, and imperfect pieces, or seconds, are usually thrown into a reject pile. For many projects these rejects are precisely what you're looking for, and the price is often easily negotiated.

Another good source is your city or county forester. He or she knows what's going on and who's doing it when it comes to logging and lumbering.

DRYING GREEN OR FRESH-SAWED LUMBER

One simple process for drying green lumber is to stack fresh-cut boards in stickered piles and let them air-dry outside (Illus. 33–35). This method does not produce good quality indoor furniture wood. When dried this way for a year or so, however, it can be moved indoors for another conditioning period of three to six months, which should be done before working it into indoor furniture, panelling, and so on. Air-dried one-inch softwood is suitable for working after allowed to air-dry for three to six months (Illus. 34). Two-inch stock takes twice as long or longer to dry. Two-inch cedar dries relatively faster than many other species and can often be used for some jobs in less than a year. Other two-inch softwoods may require 18 to 24 months to dry before they are ready to be worked.

Illus. 33. Stickering a pile of lumber for air-drying. The sticks provide air spaces between each layer.

Illus. 34. This pile of air-drying lumber is roofed with waterproof building paper (weighted down) to shed rain and snow.

Illus. 35. Our "stockyard" of fresh-cut 2-inch white cedar, air-drying in stacks.

FIREWOOD

Firewood is usually easy to obtain. Weekend treks into the forest are sure to produce something of value (Illus. 36). Dead branches, which make good carving and turning chunks, are often found well elevated and dry.

Spalted wood (Illus. 37), with its diverse grain pattern, is another good find. Spalting is caused by a fungus that grows in wet wood at temperatures between 70 °F and 100 °F. A white-rot fungus produces successive layers of dark lines that outline and surround the area of growth, making beautiful patterns in the wood (Illus. 38).

Illus. 36. Firewood piles often contain good pieces for turning or carving.

Illus. 37. Spalted designs are frequently found in wood that has been in wet and warm areas.

Illus. 38. This free-form carving by Don Jackson is another vivid example of the patterns formed by spalting.

SLABS AND SLICES

You can cut slabs and slices of various types (Illus. 39–40) with a chain saw. You may also want to consider treating fresh-cut (green) wood with polyethylene glycol 1000 (PEG). Refer to my earlier book *Working Green Wood with PEG* for illustrations of and instructions on making several rustic objects (Illus. 41). Because that book covered the subject in detail, I have avoided duplicating information here.

Illus. 39. A flat-cut slab (a) and a diagonal-cut slab (b).

Illus. 40. Cutting a full cross-sectioned end-grain slab. (Photograph courtesy of Homelite.)

Illus. 41. Unusual lamp base treated with PEG.

RECYCLING WOOD

Construction sites, demolition projects, landfills, parks, vacant lots, rural areas such as fence lines, pastures, barnyards, old buildings, and similar locations often contain prized findings (Illus. 42–43) for unique projects (Illus. 44–45). Boards, lumber, and the popular "barn wood" that have been weathered grey make unusual pots, like the ones fashioned from fence posts in Illus. 46 and 47. Old barn boards (Illus. 48–49) were used to make the chest shown in Illus. 50 and Color Illus. A1. Consider using framing members from old or dismantled buildings for your projects. After all, this material has dried for many, many years. So what if the surfaces of this recycled lumber are rust-stained from nail holes? You can insert a filler into the holes and sand the surface to produce an interesting, artistic effect. And, if the wood is rough-sawn, which it often is in old buildings, so much the better; touch sanding will make it very attractive. Certainly, used wood (Illus. 51) with its distinctive markings could never be confused with imitation wood, such as plastic or vinyl reproductions.

SHEET MATERIALS

Large plywoodlike panels facilitate the construction of many items. The backs of gun cabinets, bars, sides for cabinets, and cabinet doors can often be made from sheet stock or panelling (Illus. 52–53).

Illus. 42. A pile of weathered lumber and boards in a vacant lot.

Illus. 43. Old, weathered logs and squared posts make attractive rustic projects such as those in Illus. 44 and 45.

Illus. 44. A planter made from an 8 × 8: the hole was band-sawed out, the kerf glued closed, and a plywood bottom was rabbeted and nailed into place.

Illus. 45. This popular one-half log rustic bench can be made from any log 8 inches and larger in diameter. Height should be approximately 17 inches.

Illus. 46. Another of Don Jackson's fence-post weed pots. Note the weathered surfaces and fencing staple left untouched.

Illus. 47. Note how the aged cracks and knot add to the charm of Don Jackson's carving.

Illus. 48. Weathered boards (barn wood) have a distinct quality. In front is a slab cut from a weathered fence post.

Illus. 49. (Above) Reclaimed, weathered drop siding. (Below) Same material with the edges trimmed off.

Illus. 50. This handsome barn-wood chest (approximately 20" × 44" × 17" with a 4-inch toeboard) was made by Bob Schultz with a professionally upholstered pad on a barn-wood–edged, plywood, lid-type seat.

Illus. 51. Old, worn, and dirty boards, which can be worked into unusual projects, have a lot of character.

Plywood can be obtained with brushed, grooved, and saw-textured surfaces with both band-sawed (Illus. 52) and circular-sawed (Illus. 53) effects.

Wafer board (slices of wood that have been bonded together) is an economical, strong, and usually weatherproof material. Use it for the backs and bottoms of cabinetry and areas not readily visible.

Illus. 52. Sheet materials: wafer board and rough-sawn cedar plywood.

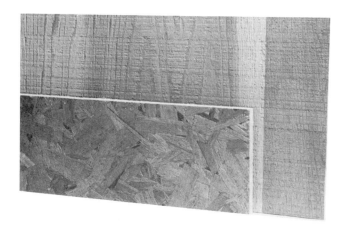

Illus. 53. This rough, circular-sawn effect on plywood siding has been an old favorite for a number of years. (Photograph courtesy of U.S. Plywood Corp.)

CEDAR SHINGLES, SHAKES, AND FENCE POSTS

Commercially made shingles can be used for panelling a room or an exterior, or they can be placed over low-cost panelling, such as wafer board. Shingles also make interesting furniture and cabinet panels (Illus. 309). For interior projects be sure to explore the possibility of obtaining the cheapest available grades. Since they are only decorative, look for the thin cuts of No. 3 or No. 4 undercoursing shingles, which are more interesting than clear, No. 1 grades because of their various blemishes. Refer to page 72 for instructions on cutting your own shingles in any size for various projects.

Many lumberyards sell cedar fence posts, which are reasonably priced. Use them for turning cylinders; slab or cut them into shingles with a band saw; saw them into crosscut discs for various end-grain slab applications. See Illus. 206 on page 91 for a panel that was made from cross-sectional discs.

Ask your local building products supplier for assistance. He may want to unload some unusual products from his inventory. Crates and crating, old or discarded furniture and cabinetry often contain salvageable material. Anything from an old board fence to a tree branch could provide material for one of your projects.

2 Hand Tools and Power Tools

In the hands of a skilled craftsman, hand tools can perform most of the work necessary for many of the projects. Hand saws, hand planes, hand drills, a selection of squares and measuring tools, plus screwdrivers, hammers, and other basic fastening (or dismantling) tools are the basic essentials for country-rustic furniture making. For shaping, forming, and texturing, you will need chisels and files. When you advance to the larger projects, you will need power tools and clamps (Illus. 54–55) for gluing large panels and assembling pieces. If you are highly skilled, make gluing surfaces smooth and make rough-cut boards even and uniformly thick with a hand plane. These

Illus. 54. Use bar clamps for gluing boards edge to edge to make wider panels and for assembling projects. (Photograph courtesy of Adjustable Clamp Co.)

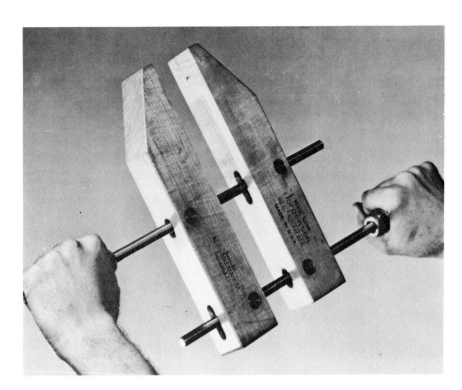

Illus. 55. Use wooden hand-screw clamps for a variety of gluing jobs; they also serve as a good work-holding tool. (Photograph courtesy of Adjustable Clamp Co.)

jobs can also be done easily with a jointer (Illus. 56) and a power planer (Illus. 57), respectively.

Use a power-driven table circular saw (Illus. 58) for straight-line sawing and joinery cuts. Although some straight-line sawing can be done with a hand-held electric sabre saw (Illus. 59), this saw is better for cutting irregular curves. For cutting curves, discs, and for rough-texturing of thick boards, a band saw (Illus. 60) is best. Likewise, a drill press (Illus. 61) is much more convenient than a hand drill or a hand-held power drill (Illus. 62). The drill press is used for drilling, boring, and sanding. Extensive sanding is not required for making country-rustic furniture, but power sanders (Illus. 63–64) make the job much easier.

Finally, the router is a tremendously versatile tool. It can be used for a variety of edge-forming jobs (Illus. 65) and for making joint cuts and templates. For more ideas about router production and duplication jobs, jigs, fixtures, and so on, refer to my *Router Handbook* (Sterling Publishing Co., 1983).

Hand tools and power tools both are expensive. To keep costs down, rent, borrow, or barter for the tools you lack.

If you are unfamiliar with the tools mentioned here, consult the local library for books on basic tool use and safety.

Illus. 56. Prepare board edges for gluing into panels with a small jointer.

Illus. 57. A thickness planer is very useful for working rough-sawn stock to uniform thickness. For most projects the face side is left rough-sawn, and the back (second) side only is planed.

Illus. 58. A table saw makes straight-line ripping and crosscutting easy. It also produces joint-fitting cuts quickly and accurately.

Illus. 59. A portable electric sabre saw is useful for some straight-line cutting and for sawing irregular curves in boards and planks. (Photograph courtesy of Black & Decker.)

Illus. 60. A band saw cuts straight and irregular curves in thin or thick material and also surface-textures.

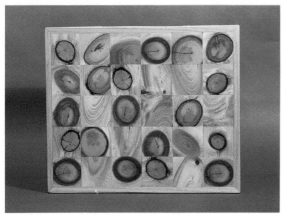

1. *Weathered barn-wood chest with upholstered seat (p. 27).*

2. *Insect tunnelling design (p. 43).*

3. *Bird feeder of rough-sawn wood and shingles (p. 72).*

5. *Mosaic panel of pine knots (p. 91).*

4. *Nightstand of weathered barn boards (p. 82).*

A

7. Rustic plant stands and weed pots (p. 115).

6. Wood Works' entrance, mailbox, walkway, shingled siding (pp. 98, 101).

8. Example of drum-sander texturing (p. 117).

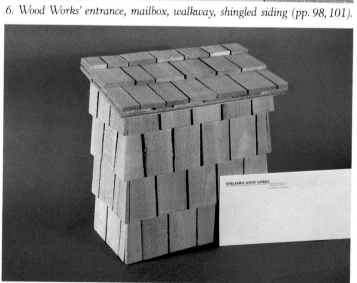

9. Minishingled, wall-mounted mailbox (p. 132).

10. Mailbox with paper tube (p. 127).

B

11. Gun cabinet of rough-sawn boards and shingles (p. 137).

12. Wood box from painted barn boards (p. 143).

13. Table with plastic pipe legs (p. 146).

14. Rough 2 × 4's and dowels make an easy table (p. 145).

15. *2½-foot rocker, round table, and 4-foot bench rocker (p. 155).*

16. *4-foot round table and stool set (p. 148).*

17. *4-foot round table set (p. 149).*

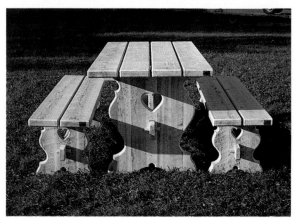

18. *Picnic table set (p. 153).*

19. *5-foot swing with arms (p. 156).*

D

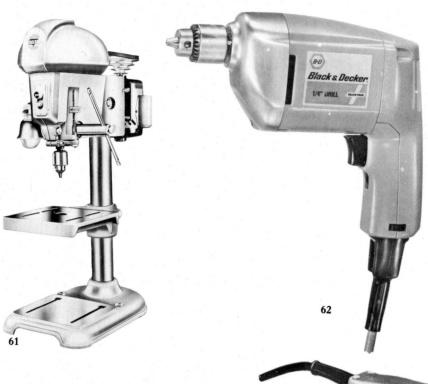

61

62

Illus. 61. In addition to making holes in wood, a drill press can perform a variety of other tasks.

Illus. 62. An inexpensive portable electric drill is usually a standard tool for most woodworkers.

Illus. 63. Use a power belt sander for touch-sanding rough-sawn surfaces. This highlights texturing made by the mill saws, and touch sanding removes any dangerous slivers or protruding fibres.

63

64

Illus. 64. Pad-type sanders are also capable of handling any required sanding job. (Photograph courtesy of Milwaukee Electric Tool Corp.)

Illus. 65. An underneath view of a router cutting a chamfer.

65

3 Construction Techniques

Most of the projects in this book employ the same general construction techniques: touch sanding, band-saw texturing, edge gluing for making panels, attaching cleats, making and inserting pegs and plugs, making shingles, and some simple but unique joinery techniques. Instructions for making cabinet joints and assembly details are given in this chapter.

In addition, this chapter includes special techniques, such as simulating hand-hewn surfaces and putting square pegs into round holes. None of these techniques is new or revolutionary, but some are original to Spielmans Wood Works. You may find that many of these techniques can be modified and incorporated into your own designs. All of the techniques, however, are ideally suited to making and assembling the projects based on our plans—those included in this book and those listed on page 159 (available by mail only).

SURFACE TEXTURING

Touch sanding. To maintain the rough-sawn appearance of the wood, sand only lightly over the entire exposed surface. A belt sander is the best tool (Illus. 66). This touch sanding cuts off fibres that often extend above the surface as shown in Illus. 67. Areas around knots, especially, require sanding to eliminate dangerous splinters that are too rough for furniture surfaces. Another important reason for touch sanding is to highlight mill saw marks on the surface.

Most softwoods do not have particularly interesting grain patterns (figures) when surfaced smooth. Sanding lightly with a belt sander improves the workability of rough-sawn boards and planks. Such even, lightly sanded surfaces enable the board to move easily through and over machinery tables. Touch sanding is normally done only to the board's face—the side exposed to the eye and to the weather. Touch

Illus. 66. Belt sanding with coarse abrasives highlights mill saw marks and levels protruding fibres or slivers. The result is a rough, rustic look, but the feel is remarkably smooth.

Illus. 67. Knots and surrounding grain are usually very rough.

sanding helps to level and reduce any existing cupping (warpage). Remember, to achieve the most interesting surface texture and the most serviceable exterior surface, place the bark side up of boards and planks instead of the pith, or tree-center, side. Plane the backside smooth. This will ensure that the surfaced stock will be uniform in thickness.

Band-saw texturing. Should the stock you have not be rough-sawn, you can texture it yourself with a band saw (Illus. 68–69). Feed the board backwards along the side of the saw blade so that the teeth just "skin" the surface. If you feed it almost parallel to the cutting direction of the blade, you will remove a thin layer from the surface. By feeding it so the stock contacts the blade at more of an oblique angle, you will remove more stock and produce a deeper texture. Texture or skin wide boards and planks at feeding angles that are more oblique to the blade. Texture wider surfaces on a band saw with a wide, rather than a narrow, blade (Illus. 69).

The recommended abrasive grits for touch sanding vary according to the depth of the roughened surfaces made by the mill saw or your band saw. Very coarse abrasive grits can quickly remove the markings made by your band-saw texturing. To touch-sand your own band-saw textured surfaces, you should sand very lightly with fine grades, such as 100- to 150-grit abrasives. Pad sanders (Illus. 70) do not cut as fast as belt sanders do and will not remove shallow texturing quickly. Establish your own system for the degree of roughness you want.

Illus. 68. Band-saw texturing a 2 × 4. The stock is fed backwards against the blade with a minimum of sideways pressure so that you just "skin" the surface with the side of the blade.

Illus. 69. Band-saw texturing a 2 × 6 plank. Note that a wider blade is used and that the feed direction is more oblique—not as parallel to the side of the blade.

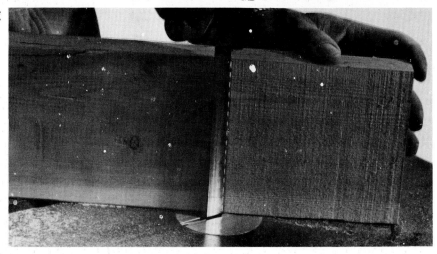

I always sand with 50- or 60-grit aluminum oxide abrasives for fast cutting. All of my stock, however, comes cut by band mills or mill circular saws, which produce very rough-textured surfaces. I texture with a band saw only those surfaces, such as table-sawn (ripped) edges, that must match rough-sawn faces. Incidentally, at Spielmans Wood Works we have experimented with rough-sawn texturing on the table saw. To get a roughened table-saw cut, we set one tooth considerably more outward than the others on the same blade. Although this cut is rougher than the cut produced by normal sawing, there are some disadvantages: the stock cannot be controlled easily in feeding and the texturing is not as spectacular or as safely accomplished as that done by a band saw.

Edge treatments. Straight and true edges often look monotonous. By rasping, draw-knifing, or sanding (Illus. 71–73), you can make a board or plank look more interesting, more like a handcrafted piece. Texturing with a carving gouge produces a rustic look to edges and other surfaces (Illus. 74–76). Sand lightly with fine abrasives to highlight the tooled texturing.

Hand hewing. This process can be accomplished quickly and effectively on either rough-sawn or smooth boards and planks. This process might be applied to beams and posts or even to some furniture items. A bar in your recreation room or planked shelving and doors are just a few objects that might be enhanced with hewn surfaces. Follow the simple steps outlined in Illus. 78–81.

Charring. Another simple but effective texturing and surface-finishing technique is achieved with a torch (Illus. 82). This process is ideal

Illus. 71. Produce a worn or aged look by randomly rasping the edges.

Illus. 72. A drawknife cuts away the edges and produces the same effect.

Illus. 73. The interesting edge texturing of this clock was accomplished with a drum sander. (See Illus. 258 on page 116.)

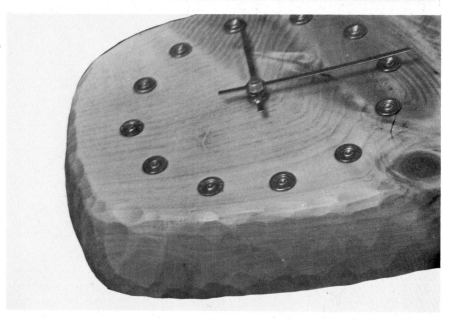

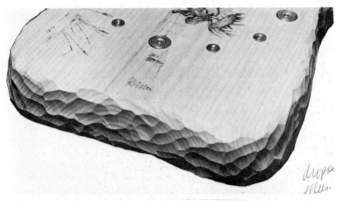

Illus. 74. The edges of this slab clock were textured with a wood-carver's gouge. (See pages 116–17 for other clock designs.)

Illus. 75. A rough-sawn plank that has been hand-carved into a tray.

Illus. 76. A closer look at the surfaces of the gouge-carved tray. After carving it was given a light sanding with fine abrasive only. It was then finished with a saturating application of peanut oil.

Illus. 77. A round-over bit when attached to the router quickly makes sliver-free edges for plank furniture.

Illus. 78. Make deep, randomly spaced, cross-grain incisions with a hatchet.

Illus. 79. Use an inshave to work the entire surface. Large wood chisel, adze, or hatchet will also work.

Illus. 80. If the edge will be exposed, work it in the same manner.

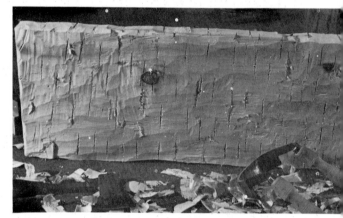

Illus. 81. A completely hewn plank. Authentic-looking, isn't it?

Illus. 82. Torching burns away the soft, less dense areas of the growth rings, creating ridges along the natural lines of the wood.

for disguising cheap, easily recognizable wood species, like fir. The best kinds of wood for this process are those with alternating hard and soft growth rings. Douglas fir and cedar planks produce some of the best effects. End-grain growth rings in Douglas fir are highlighted in Illus. 83. Western red and Northern white cedar, white fir, and Southern pine respond to this technique fairly well. Fast-grown Douglas fir, however, is best because of its accentuated patterns.

Be sure to do the charring far from other flammable materials. Keep a fire-extinguisher, a water bucket, and a wet rag on hand. Once you have completed the torching, let the work cool. Then remove the charred surfaces with a wire brush (Illus. 84) or stiff bristle brush, like one used to shine shoes. For wood that is softer overall than fir and cedar with their alternating hard and soft growth rings, use coarse steel wool (Illus. 85). Hardware suppliers sell rotary

Illus. 83. This charred Douglas fir end grain shows the dramatic effects of the charring technique.

Illus. 84. A soft-wire brush removes the softer, charred areas between the growth lines of the wood. For woods that are soft overall, use a bristle shoeshine-type brush (shown in the foreground) or coarse steel wool as shown in Illus. 85.

wire brushes in different degrees of bristle stiffness. When mounted on an electric drill, these brushes make removing the necessary materials easier. Don't be concerned with the appearance of fine checks or cracks; they simply add to the overall handmade effect. See Illus. 86–88 for objects that have been band-sawn, turned, carved, and textured by charring.

Illus. 85. Use steel wool after charring. Then wipe with an old rag or terry to remove the fine particles.

Illus. 86. Weed pots of charred Douglas fir shaped by compound band sawing (far right) and lathe turning.

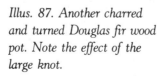

Illus. 87. Another charred and turned Douglas fir wood pot. Note the effect of the large knot.

Illus. 88. Simple carvings are also enhanced by charring. Avoid carving fine details, which would only become obscured by the burning process.

After you have worked the charred areas to your satisfaction, wipe the remaining "fines" (soot residue) away with an old bath towel or terry rag. Then finish the surfaces or leave them. The easiest finishing method is to spray or brush on a clear, satin finish or apply two coats of spray-on furniture polish. Another method is to apply a stain (dark) and then to add numerous layers of finish to create a durable surface. Indoor furniture, like bars and table tops, benefits from such protective finishes.

Some of the most appealing surface texturing is performed by Mother Nature. We need to learn how to recognize her incredibly canny designs and incorporate them into our own. The lamp base in Illus. 89 is enhanced by making the voided knot its focal point. The paths in Illus. 90 and Color Illus. A2 were made by feeding larvae as they tunnelled under the bark of a cedar. When dried, the bark fell away, revealing another example of nature's artistic texturing. The grubs have long since exited, leaving only their pathways as evidence of their earlier life under the bark. This unusual container was hollowed out with a band saw and then the kerf—created so that the

Illus. 89. This turning in wormy butternut also features a dead knot void.

Illus. 90. Tunnelling paths of grub worms feeding under the bark of a cedar created this artistic texturing.

Illus. 91. A vivid example of the protection paint provides against weathering. Over the many years of exposure, only the painted letters resisted deterioration and have gradually become raised in relief with a naturally textured background.

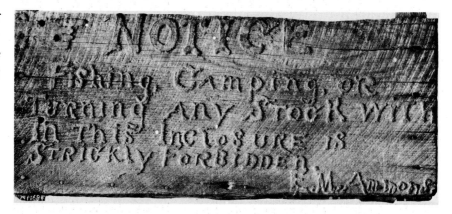

blade could enter and exit the log's center—was reglued. A plywood disc was cut to fit the bottom and glued in place.

The weather also has a slow, natural texturing effect on wood surfaces. Authorities state that unfinished or unprotected wood wears away at a rate of about ¼ inch every 100 years (Illus. 91). Weather-worn texturing looks like char-texturing because over the years the soft areas of growth rings wear away faster than the remaining wood.

GLUING PANELS

Different kinds of panels can be made by gluing together the edges of two or more narrow boards or planks. You can either hide the glue joint (Illus. 92) or accentuate it (Illus. 93). Panels with accentuated glue joints are made by gluing together boards that have chamfered edges, which produces the **V** shape along the joint.

Glued-up panelling alleviates problems that occur when using one large board. First of all, very wide boards are normally not available. Although various kinds of plywoods can be used for large surfaces, they do not produce the same effect as edge-glued boards do. Even if very wide boards were available, they would probably warp or cup. Should extra-wide solid boards be available, you should still rip them into narrower boards and then reglue them. For a 1 × 10 board, rip it into two 5-inch pieces and then glue them back together. Ripping relieves the internal stresses within wide boards and thus minimizes subsequent warping.

Common practice for gluing panels is to alternate the pith and bark sides of the boards in the panel. At Spielmans Wood Works, however, we always choose the best-looking side and place it face up. This is usually the bark side (Illus. 94). Some of our panels do warp, but alternating pith and bark sides is too time-consuming and produces inferior-looking panels.

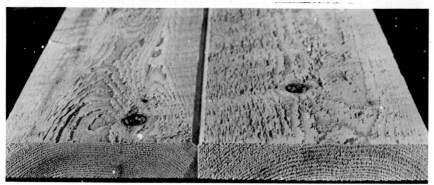

Illus. 92. A finished panel of four rough-sawn boards glued edge to edge and touch sanded.

Illus. 93. Another style of glued-up panelling. Each board has slightly chamfered edges, which make a V at the joint. Glue runout is, therefore, easier to clean up.

Illus. 94. By looking at the end grain you can see that these boards are bark side up. In conventional panel making the pith and bark sides alternate throughout.

Most of our panels are made from thick (2-inch), narrow (not more than 6-inch-wide) planks (Illus. 95). Usually the stock ranges between 3 and 5 inches wide. See the finished bench end in Illus. 96.

Making large panels with rough-sawn faces poses problems different from those inherent in gluing together smooth boards or planks. Rough-sawn surfaces make it difficult to completely wipe away glue that squeezes out of a joint or the glue that may fall onto the surfaces. Panels with chamfered edges make glue removal at the joint much easier. If you are not careful, however, glue will probably seep into various pockets of the rough surfaces. For this reason, use a glue that is easy to clean up and that dries to a woodlike color. Outdoor furniture requires a quality waterproof glue. Most authorities recommend resorcinol-formaldehyde or epoxies for waterproof glue joints. I see disadvantages in both. Resorcinols leave wide, ugly red lines, and epoxies are hard to clean up. Both are very expensive.

Illus. 95. A typical panel glue-up prior to final touch sanding. Note the narrow widths of the individual pieces.

Illus. 96. A glued-up panel worked into a bench end.

Illus. 97. Glue.

We've had exceptionally good luck with a marine-grade plastic resin (Illus. 97) that is far more economical. It is available in powder form, and it mixes and cleans up with water. Depending upon the temperature, the plastic resin sets in three to four hours and cures in 12 hours. This glue works well with Western red and white cedar. For over ten years we have used it for exterior wood signs, outdoor furniture of all types, wood mailboxes, and posts. Not one customer has ever returned a product or complained of joint failure.

Be sure to test your choice of glue with the species of wood you most commonly use. Almost any glue, including the ready-to-use liquid white or the liquid yellow, is suitable for indoor projects. When gluing together pieces for any project, make sure you wipe off all excess, or runout, with warm water before the glue sets.

To prepare and glue boards for panels, follow these routine woodworking steps. First, establish the type and size panel you want to make. Then plane the boards (planks) to uniform thickness and plane the edges square. If you want to chamfer the edges, use a router with a chamfer bit or plane the edges by hand (Illus. 98). Ensure the gluing order by chalking the boards as shown in Illus. 99.

Hold the pieces together and check them along their length for bowing. Wherever the edges do not align at the face (Illus. 100) is a good indication of where you should place a dowel. Some woodworkers spline their joints (Illus. 101). This is an effective table saw

Illus. 98. Chamfering edges with a hand plane.

Illus. 99. Plan and arrange the boards as desired within the panel. To prevent the boards from becoming mixed up, draw a triangle, as shown.

Illus. 100. Plan to place dowels where boards do not align uniformly along the face edges. Note how this one is warped up lengthwise from the one next to it.

technique if the boards are straight and you can do the job accurately. But it is sometimes difficult to accomplish if the board has any distortion along its length. Splines are more complicated to machine unless you allow them to run all the way through the panel, exiting (and visible) at both ends. If you have a good centering jig, you should dowel it instead (Illus. 102). Place the dowels only where necessary. Dowels are easier to hide within the panel than splines. Although dowels or splines help to align the pieces during clamping, they probably do not add any significant strength to an edge-glued joint. If the gluing surfaces are cut cleanly and fit tightly, the glue line will be stronger than the surrounding wood. The remaining steps are shown in Illus. 103–111. Also see Illus. 113.

Illus. 101. (Left) A table-saw–cut plywood spline joint and (right) a dowel joint.

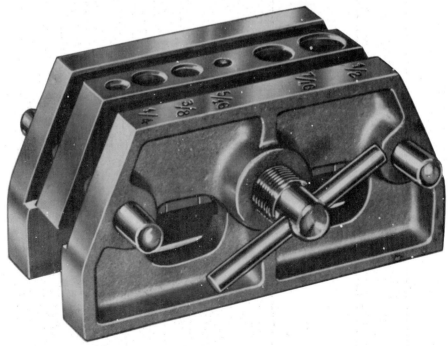

Illus. 102. A self-centering dowel jig makes locating and drilling holes easy.

Illus. 103. Mark both surfaces of the joint to identify dowel locations.

Illus. 104. Drilling dowel holes. Note the stop block under the drill chuck, which limits hole depth.

Illus. 105. Spreading the glue. Don't worry about getting glue into holes or onto dowel pins.

Illus. 106. Drive dowels into one member of the joint.

Illus. 107. A panel in the clamps. Note the placement of clamps alternating above and below the panel.

Illus. 108. A closeup look at glue squeezeout.

Illus. 109. Use a putty knife to scrape out excess glue. Always use a lifting action to avoid driving glue down into the rough-cut surfaces.

Illus. 110. Wipe up carefully with a water-dampened rag. When dry, touch-sand lightly once more.

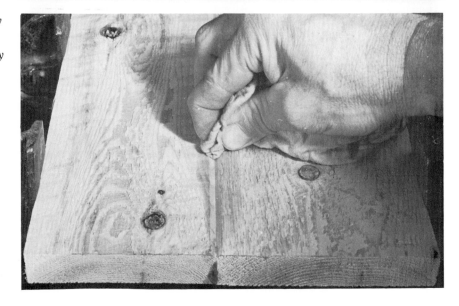

Illus. 111. There is little evidence of glue remaining on the rough-textured surfaces of a nice, tight, clean joint.

MORE JOINTS AND PANELS

See Illus. 112 for other easy-to-make joints and study Illus. 113 for joints and assembly techniques used in basic cabinetry. Refer to page 137 for more cabinet construction details.

Mitre joints. Rough-sawn woods are easy to edge-mitre. By employing a trick or two of the trade, you can produce an almost invisible glue line (Illus. 114). Edge-mitred joints like these are used to make fake box beams and hollow posts. This joint can also be useful in furniture making. If done carefully this technique can be employed to join or "box" thin, 1-inch boards to simulate thick, heavy boards.

First bevel-rip the pieces on the table saw (Illus. 115) and prepare the edges to be glued. Then glue the pieces together and secure them with nails so the glue sets properly (Illus. 116). If you object to nail holes, tape the mitre joint (Illus. 117–121).

Metal-splined mitre joints. Clamp nails are thin, tapered metal fasteners. Inserted somewhat like splines, they facilitate some otherwise difficult jointing tasks (Illus. 122–123). Clamp nails are designed to draw or clamp together the two pieces as you hammer them in (Illus. 124).

First, cut a narrow kerf into the board's edge with a thin, 22-gauge circular saw blade (Illus. 125). Then glue and join the edges. Before the glue dries, hammer in the clamp nail. The sides of the clamp nail are flanged (Illus. 123–124) with sharp edges that cut into wood fibres as they are driven in (Illus. 126). Clamp-nailed joints, unlike wood-splined joints, are less likely to separate as a result of expansion and contraction. To set a clamp nail below the surface (Illus. 127), grind away the flanges of a second clamp nail, turn it upside down, and hammer it down ½ inch to 1 inch on top of the first clamp nail. Remove the second clamp nail. To fill in the resulting hole and conceal the first clamp nail, glue a thin, ripped edging into the kerf (Illus. 128–129).

Clamp nails also nicely secure end-mitre joints (Illus. 130) for boxes, furniture, and cabinet toeboards. Cut the kerfs with the table saw blade tilted at a 45° angle. Feed the stock along the mitre gauge with the end against the fence, as shown in Illus. 131.

Illus. 112. Some basic right-angle joints.

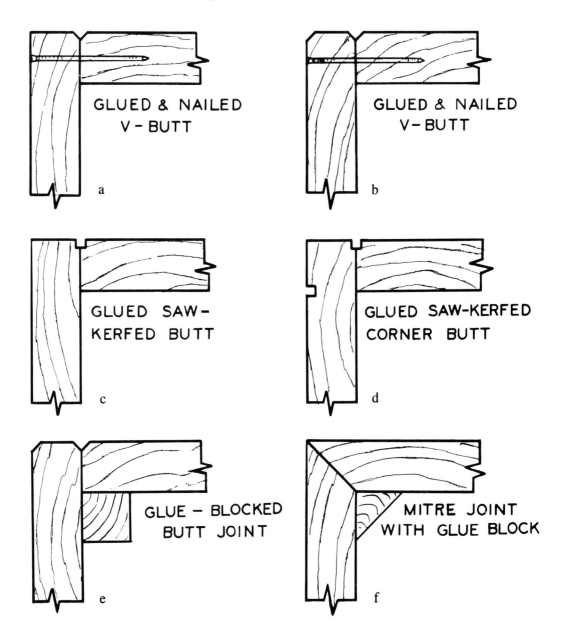

GLUED & NAILED V-BUTT

a

GLUED & NAILED V-BUTT

b

GLUED SAW-KERFED BUTT

c

GLUED SAW-KERFED CORNER BUTT

d

GLUE – BLOCKED BUTT JOINT

e

MITRE JOINT WITH GLUE BLOCK

f

Illus. 113. A rear view of a cabinet in process illustrates a glued V-joint panel, cabinet facing, glue-block applications, and a rabbeted-in-plywood back panel.

Illus. 114. An edge-mitre joint of rough-sawn wood.

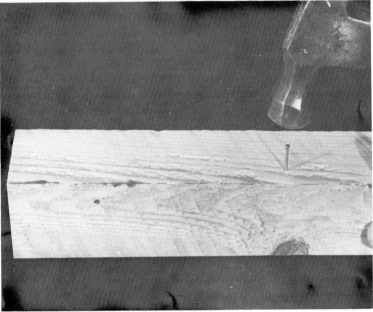

Illus. 116. Nailing the joint.

Illus. 115. Matching up boards that have been bevel-ripped on the table saw.

Illus. 117. Tape can be used if finishing-nail holes are objectionable. The tape acts as a hinge for the assembly.

Illus. 118. Spreading the glue.

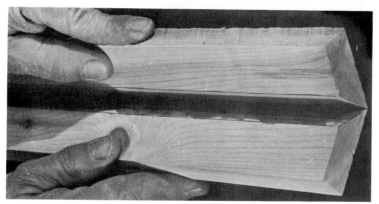

Illus. 119. Fold the joint together; the tape acts as a hinge.

Illus. 120. The joint closes tightly, releasing some glue. Wrap the tape around to hold the parts together until the glue sets.

Illus. 121. With the fibres at the "point" of the joint still soft and wet from the glue, burnish as shown to close any gaps. Sand lightly when the glue has dried.

Illus. 122. A completed edge-mitre joint held fast with a combination of glue and a metal clamp-nail spline. Note the optional V-groove joint.

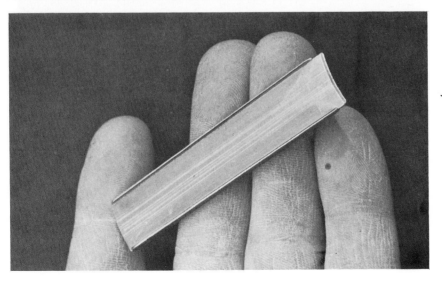

Illus. 123. A closeup look at a standard clamp nail. Note the entry end (right), which is the widest end, and the flanged edges along each side.

Illus. 124. Clamp nails.
(Left) The standard and
(right) the special flat mitre-
joint type.

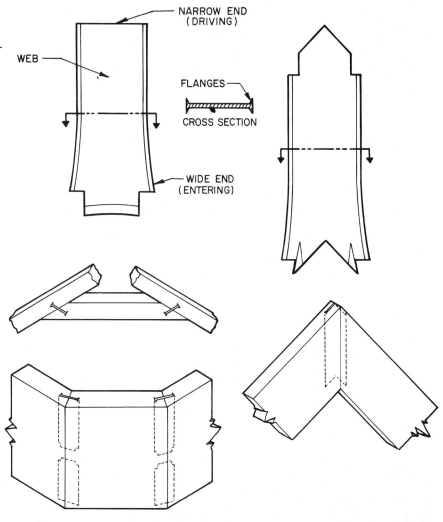

NARROW END
(DRIVING)

WEB

FLANGES

CROSS SECTION

WIDE END
(ENTERING)

Illus. 125. Narrow kerfs for
clamp nails are cut with
special, thin saw blades.

Illus. 126. Driving a clamp nail into the joint. The abutting pieces have been freshly spread with glue.

Illus. 127. Using an upside-down clamp nail from which the flanges have been removed to drive the first clamp nail below the surface.

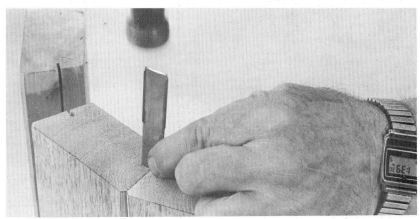

Illus. 128. A thin strip of wood is glued in to plug and conceal the second clamp nail.

Illus. 129. The completed joint is tight and very strong.

Illus. 130. An end-mitre joint, kerfed and ready for assembly with a clamp nail.

Illus. 131. This table saw setup kerfs the end mitres for clamp nailing.

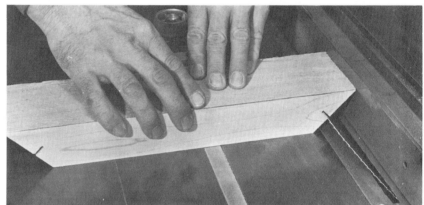

Cleats, pegs, and plugs. These make attractive accents to country-rustic furniture (Illus. 132–134) while they help keep wide panels flat and strengthen joints of all types. Both pegs and plugs hide mechanical fasteners, such as wood screws, lags, and carriage or machine bolts. Standard wooden dowels can also be used for pegs, but because the grain runs in the wrong direction, dowels that are used as plugs are difficult to work down flush to the surface.

To make pegs, carve out a series of them in an end-grain block with plug cutters (Illus. 135–136). Then measure, mark, and cut them off (Illus. 137–139). Chamfer the ends (Illus. 132 and 134) with a hand file or on a belt-sanding machine. One useful tool for plug and peg work is the adjustable counter-boring attachment (Illus. 140). It bores for the plug (or peg) and drills the screw (or bolt) hole in one operation.

Not all pegs need to be fake; they can be functional too. The unusual pegged (or pinned) lap joints in our park benches and rockers have pegs (dowel pins) running all the way through both members of the joint (Illus. 141–142).

Illus. 132. Attaching a cleat to the front of a door with panhead screws.

Illus. 133. A completed cabinet door shows functional cleats with decorative end-grain pegs.

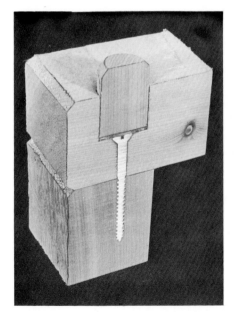

Illus. 134. Cut-away joint. Chamfered end-grain plug (peg) hides screws or bolts.

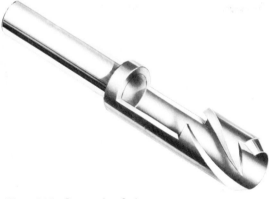

Illus. 135. One style of plug cutters.

Illus. 136. Another plug-cutting tool. Pegs, like dowel pins, are cut parallel to the grain. Plugs are usually cut against the grain.

Illus. 137. A series of end-grain dowels are cut to simulate round pegs like those in Illus. 133.

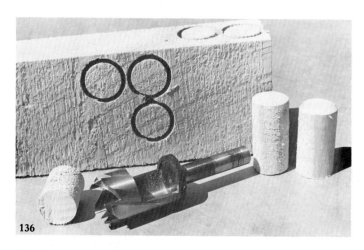

Illus. 138. Marking for cutting to the desired length.

Illus. 139. Cutting many pegs of equal length with a band saw.

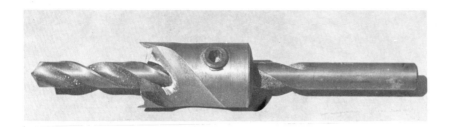

Illus. 140. A counter-boring tool drills for the screw or bolt and the plug simultaneously.

Illus. 141. Our glued and pinned lap joints are extremely strong and rugged.

Illus. 142. Our rocking chair has many pegs (pins) and plugs. The seats and back are fastened with glue and lag bolts covered with flush plugs; the arms are fastened to the seat similarly, and also with long machine bolts.

Square pegs and plugs. Joints on small projects, such as boxes and chests, can be enhanced with pegs or plugs (Illus. 143–144). Test on wood scraps before applying these devices. Avoid placing them too close to the edge or end of a board, which could cause splits to run to the end of the board.

Since the square-head pegs are driven into round holes (Illus. 144), they crush some fibres, acting like wedges. Use softwoods for both the board and the pegs, because softwood fibres compress easier than those of hardwood. Make pegs more visible by cutting them from a wood of contrasting color. You can drive pegs either below the surface, flush to the surface, or slightly above the surface (Illus. 143).

Illus. 143. Butt joint with square pegs that conceal conventional wood screws. (Top) Peg is left raised above the surface. (Center) Peg is set below the surface. (Bottom) Peg is set flush to the surface.

Illus. 144. Square pegs are rounded at their point of entry before they are glued and driven into place.

Making benches and tables. Follow the detailed procedures shown in the step-by-step photographs (Illus. 145–162) to make attractive benches, tables, and other items. Learn how to hide wood screws and lag bolts with plugs that are set flush to the surface. Make strong, enduring right-angle joints with the aid of glue blocks. My modified version of the challenging joint known as a keyed mortise-and-tenon joint is also illustrated. Using a round dowel as a "pin" wedge, rather than the conventional square-tapered wedge, to "key" the mortise-and-tenon joint simplifies this job tremendously. These same techniques, with the exception of the pinned-through mortise-and-tenon joint used in trestle tables and benches, are used to fasten back and seat planks of our park benches, bench rockers, and the seats of our swing sets. To make frames or stands for the swings, see Illus. 163–167. For information about obtaining plans for these projects, turn to page 159.

Illus. 145. A completely assembled trestle bench.

Illus. 146. The end profile shapes are cut with a band saw or sabre saw. The mortise (opening) for the stretcher tenon can be sabre-sawn or chiselled out.

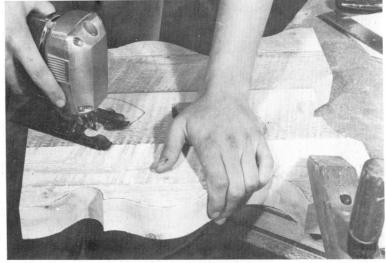

Illus. 147. The stretcher tenon is worked to fit (not too tightly) into the through mortise.

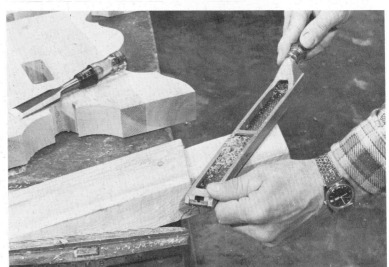

Illus. 148. Using a chisel to "knock off" the corners of the tenon.

Illus. 149. With the bench end held tightly against the shoulders of the stretcher tenon, mark the tenon as shown.

Illus. 150. Bore this 1-inch-diameter hole about 1/8 inch beyond the pencil mark.

Illus. 151. If helpful, mark the mating members of the joint on surfaces that will be hidden.

Illus. 152. The joint ready for keying (pinning). Note the edge of the hole is set back from the outer surface.

Illus. 153. The "key" to the joint is this dowel with a slight, tapered flat. Note the chamfered ends.

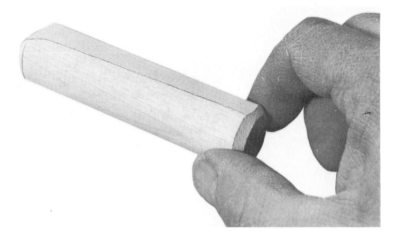

Illus. 154. Driving in the key (pin) to complete the assembly. This joint requires no glue.

Illus. 155. Seat planks that have been cut, bored, and marked for assembly.

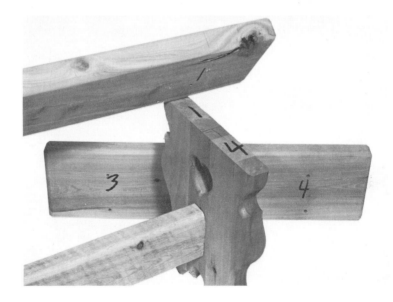

Illus. 156. Use glue on all wood-to-wood mating surfaces (except on the pinned joint in Illus. 154).

Illus. 157. Driving lag bolts to secure the seat planks to the bench ends.

Illus. 158. With glue inside the hole and on the plug, drive plug into the hole with a hammer. Be sure to align the grain of the plug with the grain of the plank.

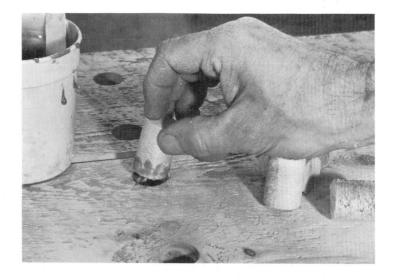

Illus. 159. Carefully cut the plugs flush to the surface with a knife or chisel.

Illus. 160. Wipe away all excess glue with a damp rag. Let the glue harden before sanding the plugged areas slightly.

Illus. 161. Glue blocks provide great additional strength.

Illus. 162. A completed trestle bench. The edges of all pieces in this version were rounded-over with a router before being assembled.

Illus. 163. After cutting the top angles of the legs and fitting them into the recesses in the top, bore holes with the pieces held as shown.

Illus. 164. Mark both mating members in each of the four joints after the holes are bored.

Illus. 165. Start the glue and bolting assembly with the pieces in the position shown.

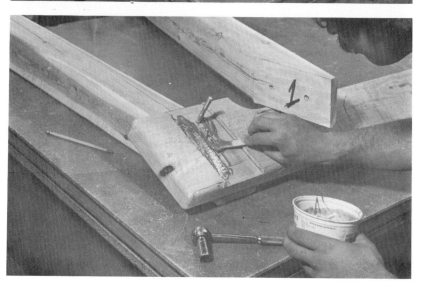

Illus. 166. The assembly is easiest when you begin with the swing frame horizontal (on its side).

Illus. 167. Stand the swing frame upright and secure all bolts. Add the pegs and let the glue cure.

Making wood shingles. Shingles of any width and less than 16 inches in length can be cut with a band saw. This is a great way to use up scraps. You can even cut up tree branches or fence posts and slice them into shingles. Shingles can be either decorative or functional (Illus. 168–169, Color Illus. A3). If you want to make shingles for exterior applications, use cedar and redwood because they weather well. Many lumberyards sell round or·square cedar and redwood fencing posts, which can be resawed into shingles (Illus. 178). Almost any species of wood can be used to make decorative shingles for indoor use (Illus. 309).

Illus. 168. A planter box made of exterior-grade plywood and covered with small shingles.

Illus. 169. Minishingles cover this bird feeder.

To make minishingles you need to construct a very simple fixture (Illus. 170–172) that slides in the table groove of a band saw. The one illustrated fits a 14-inch Delta band saw. For other brands of band saws and for saws without a table groove, modify the jig design accordingly. Or convert the jig so you can guide it against a ripping fence. If your machine is not equipped with a fence either, construct a makeshift fence by clamping a straight board to the table.

Illus. 170. This simple fixture made to slide in the table groove of a 14-inch Delta band saw is all that's needed for making minishingles.

Illus. 171. Sawing tapered shingles from 2-inch scrap. The material is turned end for end after each cut.

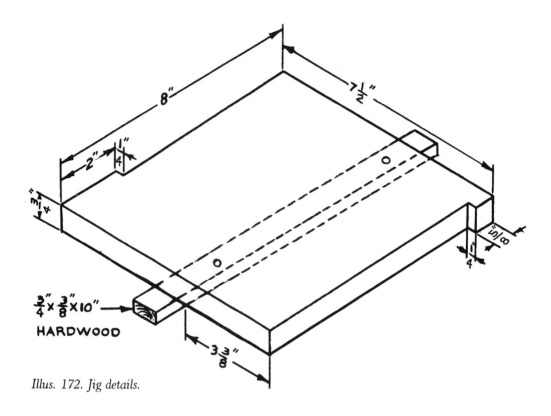

Illus. 172. Jig details.

To make tapered shingles of any width and up to 16 inches in length, or longer, construct the jig in Illus. 173–177. This jig does not work well for cutting very small shingles that are less than 6 inches long. Saw long, wide shingles with a coarse-toothed blade with big gullets, in the widest possible width. Using fairly dry material is also helpful, but not a definite requirement. If pitch gums up the blade when you cut green wood, clean it off with lacquer thinner, oven cleaner, or with a special solvent. Apply paste wax to the blade, the table, and the sliding surfaces of the fixture to help ease the operation.

The advantage of sawing your own tapered shingles is that you can experiment with natural, rustic effects. Any old chunk, tree-limb section, or weather-worn fence post will produce distinctive shingles (Illus. 178–180). Even curved log sections, crotches, pieces with knots (sound or otherwise), and logs that may be prestained or prepainted will create unusual effects. Panelling a room's walls, an entire building, or even a roof can be done very economically. Even if you purchase new shingle-making material in the better grades, the yield is so great that it is very cost-effective when compared to purchased shingles (Illus. 204 and 205).

Illus. 173. Another style jig for bigger shingle making fits a 14-inch band saw.

Illus. 174. The same jig converts scrap planks into shingles on this 20-inch band saw.

Illus. 175. Another view.

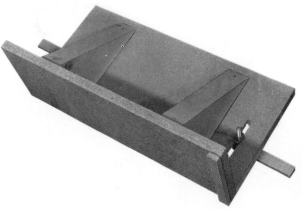

Illus. 176. The jig for sawing tapered shingles is adjustable.

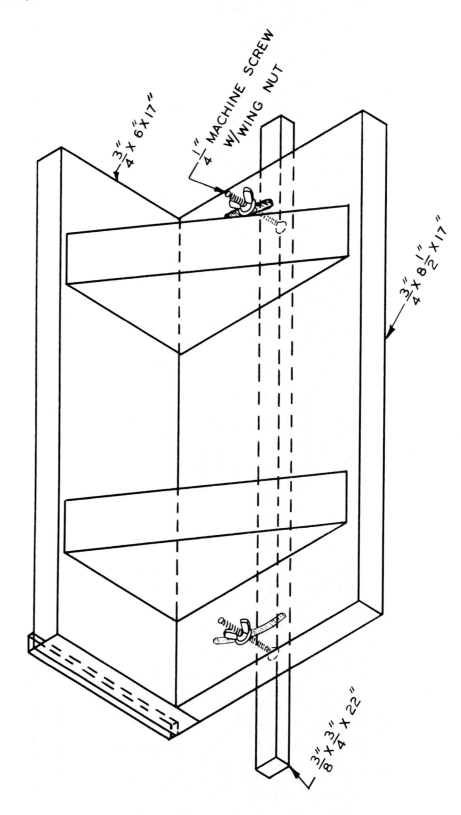

Illus. 177. Drawing of the shingle-sawing jig.

Illus. 178. A 16-inch log section and some wayne-edged slabs cut from it. Note that little material need be wasted.

Illus. 179. Normally the log is reversed (end to end) between cuts. Shingles cut side by side with their "butts" taken from the same end, however, will appear similar to each other.

Illus. 180. The safest and easiest way to start is to split (saw) the log lengthwise, approximately on center, and level the cut surfaces.

Illus. 181. Operator's view of shingle cutting.

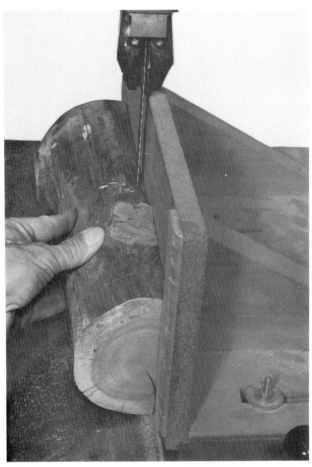

Illus. 182. Another view.

4 Finishing

This chapter covers only a few of the hundreds of ways you can finish the projects in this book. There is a lot of new information that could be written about wood finishing to accompany the abundance of material already available. As I indicated in the introduction, however, we at Spielmans Wood Works prefer to either totally eliminate or dramatically reduce tedious, time-consuming sanding (Illus. 183) and finishing. Whenever possible we don't finish the wood at all. Depending on the service expected, pegboards, picture frames, shelves, and similar items really don't need a finish. Sure, the woods may discolor with age, and they may become stained or soiled. If you're willing to accept these conditions, you don't need to apply a finish.

INTERIOR FINISHES

Indoor tables, plant stands, benches, cribbage boards, bars, and other objects that come into close human contact or are subjected to liquids should be protected. Use any of the numerous quick-drying, one-shot application finishes now on the market (Illus. 184). They are available in brush-on or aerosol dispensers. To save time I avoid

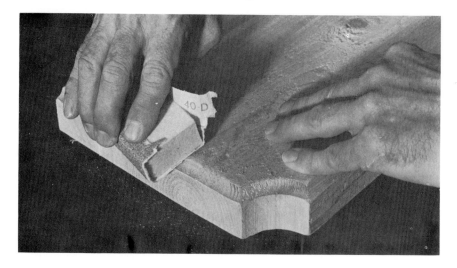

Illus. 183. Hand-sand only to soften harsh edges. Use a very coarse abrasive backed with a felt block.

Illus. 184. A combination clear sealer and top-coat natural finish will suffice for most indoor furniture.

multiple-step or multiple-coat finishes and prefer to apply a finish that combines sealer and top coat. Although I often use Danish penetrating oil finishes, which are applied in one coat, they work best on smoothly sanded wood. On rough-sawn wood, Danish oils generally produce an unattractive and unpredictable result.

Although the polymer high-gloss, wet look is currently popular, I avoid using finishes that produce this effect. Should you, however, choose them, be sure to mix those that require mixing correctly (Illus. 185–186). Polymer finishes, which are available at most good hardware dealers, produce interesting effects, especially when applied over weathered or rough-sawn wood, like the bar in Illus. 187. If you don't like the high-gloss shine, cut it with steel wool or automotive-body rubbing compound. Although this makes a great-looking, serviceable, and durable finish (Illus. 188), it is difficult to apply and fairly expensive. Check out the cost per square foot before you purchase it.

Be sure to analyze every project for the most appropriate finish, if any. Don't forget to consider the char-texturing technique described on page 37. Weathered wood (barn wood) for indoor use may not require any finish if you are satisfied with its silver-grey tone (Illus. 189, Color Illus. A4).

Incidentally, you might be interested in a little trick—the black-spray technique—I often use to match the color and texture of weathered wood (Illus. 189–192). This system works better than attempting to match a color by mixing stains. The problem with a stain is that the tone is very difficult to match exactly. The tone's intensity varies from board to board and from species to species. Because stains penetrate, they often obscure the natural, weathered look when they

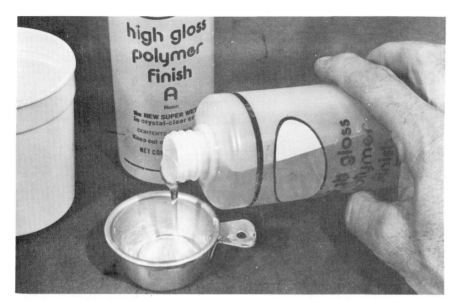

Illus. 185. Measuring the components for a polymer-type finish that produces a very high gloss.

Illus. 186. To achieve good results, be sure to follow instructions precisely for mixing the two components of the high-gloss finish and all other procedures.

seep into the weathered surface. The black-spray technique works equally well for outdoor applications, but we don't know the long-term results. In time, however, any area of exposed, "fresh" wood will probably weather naturally anyway.

Almost any finish suitable for outdoor objects can also be applied to indoor objects. Be sure the finish you choose will produce the effect you want and will not produce toxic, or persistent fumes. There are hundreds of finishes suitable for country-rustic projects. Every year something new appears on the market. Still to be developed and perfected, however, is a natural-looking finish for exterior use that lasts a lifetime.

Illus. 187. This bar top shows the perfectly clear, ultrahigh gloss produced by the two-component polymer finish.

Illus. 188. Maximum surface protection is achieved when the surface makes water bead.

Illus. 189. A little hutch (bedside stand) made of weathered boards. Notice that the sawed edges almost match the tone and color of the naturally weathered surfaces.

Illus. 190. With the fresh-sawed edge held well away, give the edge a very light dusting of flat-black spray. Be careful of the overspray, which usually is not a problem if you hold the surface (edge) perpendicular to the line of spray.

Illus. 191. Immediately sand with coarse-grit (40- to 60-grit) abrasive until you achieve just the right tone.

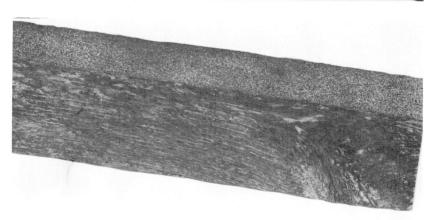

Illus. 192. The edge (upper surface) is colored to match the intensity of the naturally weathered surface.

EXTERIOR FINISHES

The so-called natural or clear finishes for exterior use must overcome the potent weathering effects of ultraviolet radiation, water, oxygen, pollutants, severe temperature changes, and also the effects of mechanical abrasion. Natural weathering of wood should not be confused with decay or rot. Decay is caused by a combination of moisture, temperature, and air. Air-dried wood will not decay if kept air-dry, and any decay that had started in the wood earlier will not progress. Wood can also be too wet for decay. If it's always water-soaked or underwater, wood will not decay because it lacks sufficient air to support the necessary fungi.

For some species of untreated wood, weathering can cause severe changes in appearance and serviceability. Some of the negative effects may include distortion and warpage, rough surfaces, checks, cracks, mildew, and color changes. But weathered wood can still provide good service and last for centuries, since the changes are only a few millimetres deep. The wood under this surface remains practically unchanged as long as it is kept free from conditions that might induce decay. Without paint or treatment of any kind, exposed wood wears away at a rate of about ¼ inch every 100 years. So, this is not a serious problem. Refer to Illus. 91.

Some woods respond more favorably than others to the effects of weathering. Softwoods, like red and white cedars, cypress, and redwood, are good choices, and they are highly decay-resistant. As the weathering process continues, wood cells on the surface turn a beautiful silver-grey color. The rate of weathering depends upon several factors, including species, natural color, and the amount of direct exposure to the sun and rain. Attempting to maintain a natural, raw-wood appearance with a coat of varnish is a mistake. Varnishes and other nonpigmented finishes seldom last over one year without cracking, turning a milky color, and separating from an often blackened wood. As a result, they don't protect the wood from intense sunrays that cause photochemical damage to the wood. If you don't want a weathered look, apply a heavily pigmented paint for long-term protection against weathering.

Apply water-repellent preservatives to raw wood to increase its longevity. Recent government restrictions, however, have made certain wood preservatives almost unobtainable beginning in February 1985. Many preservatives contain creosote, pentachlorophenol, and even arsenic ingredients. The U.S. Environmental Protection Agency has limited the sale of such chemicals because they may cause cancer. Look for nontoxic, water-repellent penetrating sealers that have wax-like ingredients and ultraviolet-light stabilizers or absorbers (Illus. 193).

Pigmented, semitransparent penetrating stains (Illus. 194) often make a good compromise between unfinished and painted wood. Available in an array of colors, these stains are easy to apply, transparent, and somewhat protective. Although the finish on horizontal surfaces of new, smooth wood lasts only two to three years, the same finish on rough-sawn woods lasts three to six years. These stains will not blister or peel, even if excessive moisture enters the wood. These sealers and stains do give a piece, like a picnic table, immediate protection from stains caused by food or beverages. Nature, however, bleaches out such stains when raw, unfinished wood is left to weather.

Illus. 193. One of the new exterior sealers and moisture repellents that penetrate deeply and are reputed to be nontoxic.

Illus. 194. Finishing a weather vane with pigmented semitransparent stain. Such products are good for either exterior or indoor items, and they work best on rough-sawn surfaces.

5 Architectural Projects

This chapter includes unusual designs (Illus. 195–223, Color Illus. A5, B6) for your home or cottage. A number of different ways to make unusual, but inexpensive, panels are illustrated and described. For the most part, they require only low-cost materials or common waste wood that are worked in various ways and then attached to or overlaid onto other inexpensive panelling materials. Incorporate the appropriate construction techniques and jigs described previously to make these panels, which can be used in small sizes for bars, cabinets, and furniture or in larger sizes for covering walls or even entire buildings.

Also included here are illustrations and plans for easy-to-make window shutters, a window-box planter, heavy rustic doors, and also plans for a wooden walkway (promenade), using pressure-treated wood.

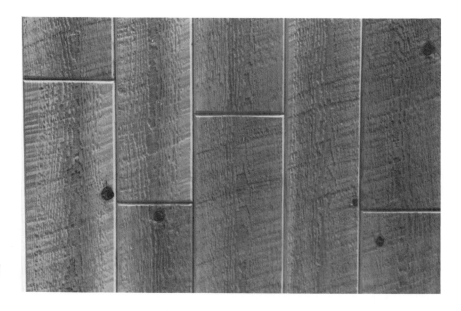

Illus. 195. One-inch rough-sawn boards, which have been touch sanded, in random widths and lengths make this beautiful textured panelling.

Illus. 196. A closeup look at the end and edge machining and how ⅛-inch hardboard splines keep all edges and ends aligned.

Illus. 197. Another look at the same panelling system.

Illus. 198. A simple but effective rustic panelling concept: 1 × 4's or 1 × 6's flat against the wall (or against a cheap panel material) are separated by 1 × 1½-inch strips set in edgewise. See Illus. 50 on page 27 and Color Illus. A1, which feature a chest made with this style of panelling.

Illus. 199. A closeup look at the rustic panelling in Illus. 198.

Illus. 200. Boards with wayne edges attached to wafer board painted black.

Illus. 201. Splined half logs make true rustic panelling.

Illus. 202. Cross-sections of splined half logs. Note chamfered bevels on edges of the cut surfaces. Use ⅛-inch or ¼-inch hardboard or plywood for splines.

Illus. 203. The flat (opposite) side of half-log panelling looks like the usual vertical board panelling.

Illus. 204. This 8 × 10-foot utility building was made of half-log construction. Shingles were band-sawn from scraps as described on page 74.

Illus. 205. An example of an interior wall covered with rustic shingles.

Illus 206. Cross-grain slices ¼ inch to ½ inch thick, cut from a dead branch and attached with panelling mastic to black-painted wafer board. The discs can be cut safely and accurately with the shingle-cutting jig to guide the work.

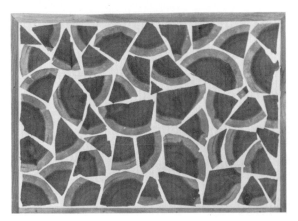

Illus. 207. Thin log-end sections attached to another backing. Spaces were filled in with white grout. Tip: prefinish wood pieces (by dipping) before gluing and grouting. Otherwise, wood will swell from the moisture in the grout and dry out later, leaving cracks.

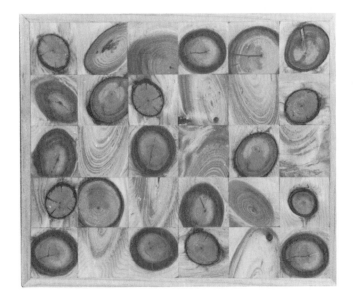

Illus. 208. Wood-knot mosaics. One-quarter-inch-thick squared knots were sawn with the shingle-cutting jig on the band saw. Individual pieces were glued to a plywood backing. See the box top in Illus. 266.

Illus. 209. Thin board-end cutoffs—about ¼-inch thick—were glued to black-painted wafer board with mastic.

Illus. 210. Detail of panel in Illus. 209.

Illus. 211. Pieces of Douglas fir that were each charred and then glued to another surface.

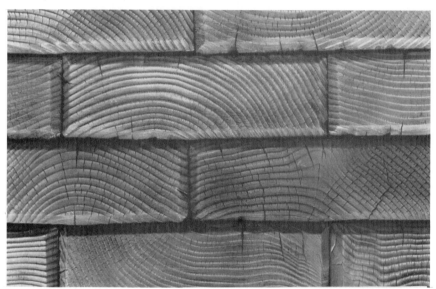

Illus. 212. Detail of Illus. 211.

Illus. 213. This window-box planter can be made to any length.

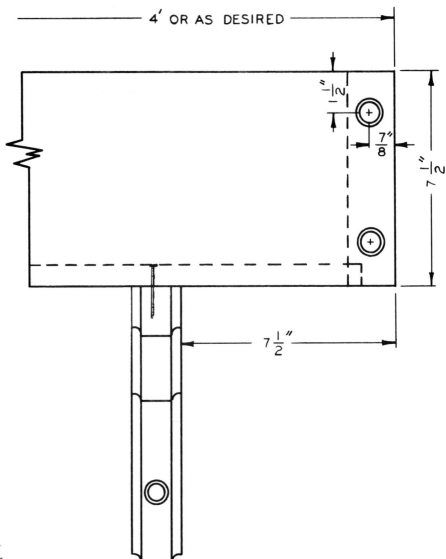

4' OR AS DESIRED

1/2"

7/8"

7 1/2"

7 1/2"

Illus. 214. Diagram.
Window-box planter.

(Plans continued next page.)

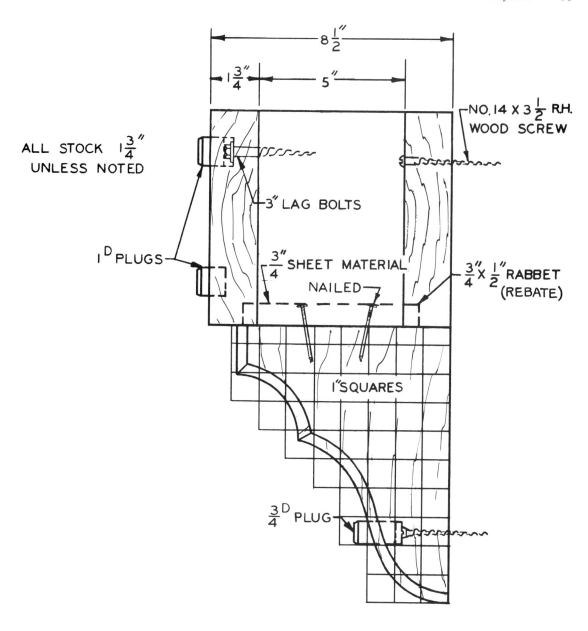

$8\frac{1}{2}''$

$1\frac{3}{4}''$ $5''$

NO. 14 X $3\frac{1}{2}$ R.H.
WOOD SCREW

ALL STOCK $1\frac{3}{4}''$
UNLESS NOTED

3" LAG BOLTS

1^D PLUGS

$\frac{3}{4}''$ SHEET MATERIAL

NAILED

$\frac{3}{4}''$ X $\frac{1}{2}''$ RABBET
(REBATE)

1" SQUARES

$\frac{3}{4}^D$ PLUG

Illus. 215. These shutters can be made in any length to fit any size window.

Illus. 216. The shutters are made simply with three pieces, edge-glued, and with pegged cleats.

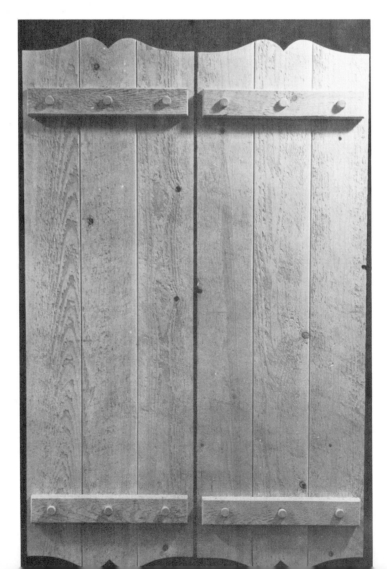

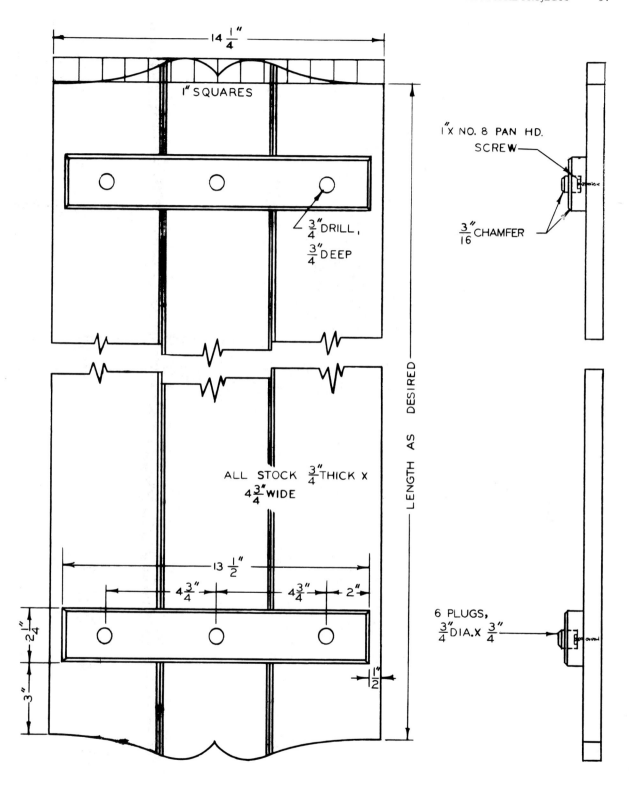

14 $\frac{1}{4}$"

1" SQUARES

$\frac{3}{4}$" DRILL,
$\frac{3}{4}$" DEEP

1" X NO. 8 PAN HD.
SCREW

$\frac{3}{16}$" CHAMFER

LENGTH AS DESIRED

ALL STOCK $\frac{3}{4}$" THICK X
4 $\frac{3}{4}$" WIDE

13 $\frac{1}{2}$"

4 $\frac{3}{4}$"   4 $\frac{3}{4}$"   2"

2 $\frac{1}{4}$"

3"

$\frac{1}{2}$"

6 PLUGS,
$\frac{3}{4}$" DIA. X $\frac{3}{4}$"

Illus. 217. Diagram. Shutter details.

Illus. 218. Heavy-plank exterior door with an opening for a custom-made, double-pane insulating insert, which can be ordered in any size from a local glass supply dealer.

Illus. 219. The Spielmans Wood Works' 3-foot plank entry door. It has a standard insulated glass insert that is available from the Visador Co. of Jasper, Texas.

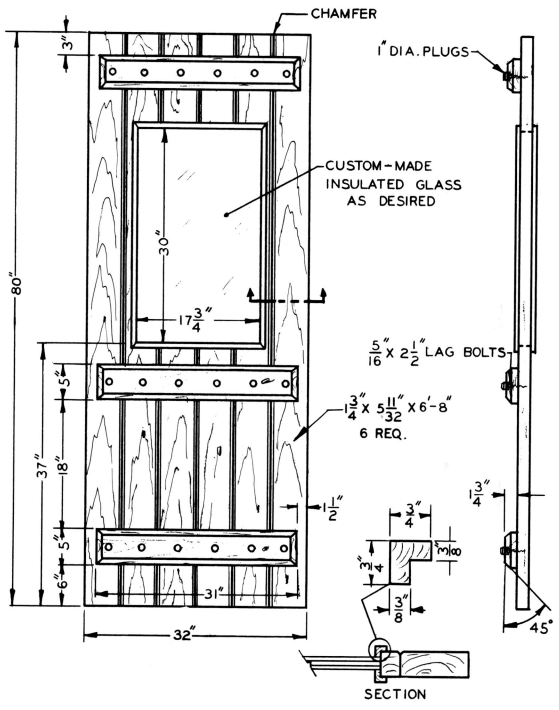

CHAMFER

1" DIA. PLUGS

CUSTOM-MADE
INSULATED GLASS
AS DESIRED

$\frac{5}{16}$" X $2\frac{1}{2}$" LAG BOLTS

$1\frac{3}{4}$" X $5\frac{11}{32}$" X 6'-8"
6 REQ.

3"

80"

30"

$17\frac{3}{4}$"

5"

37"

18"

5"

6"

31"

32"

$1\frac{1}{2}$"

$1\frac{3}{4}$"

45°

$\frac{3}{4}$"

$\frac{3}{100}$"

$\frac{3}{4}$"

$\frac{3}{4}$"

$\frac{3}{8}$"

SECTION

Illus. 220. Diagram for
exterior door in Illus. 218.
Make minor modifications as
necessary for 2-foot-6-inch
and 2-foot-10-inch doors.

(Plans continued next page.)

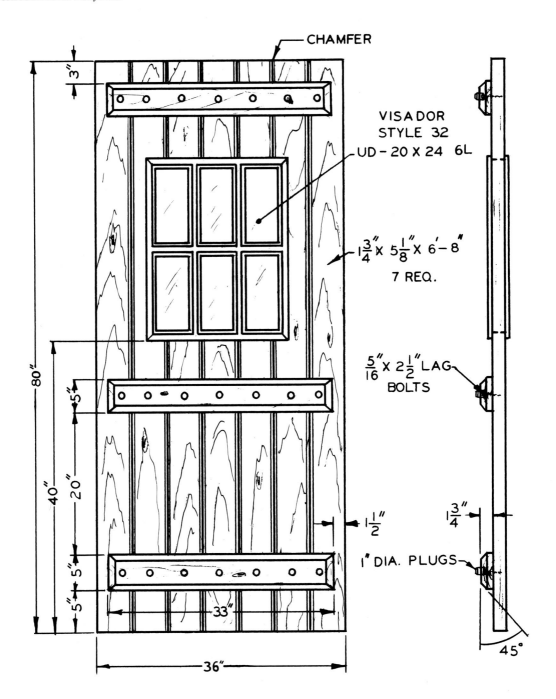

Illus. 220A. Diagram for entry door in Illus. 219.

*Illus. 221. The Wood Works'
entrance. Note the heavy
timber framing, shingled
exterior walls, and wood
plank walk.*

*Illus. 222. Wooden
walkways.*

Illus. 223. Diagram.
Construction details of
wooden walkways.

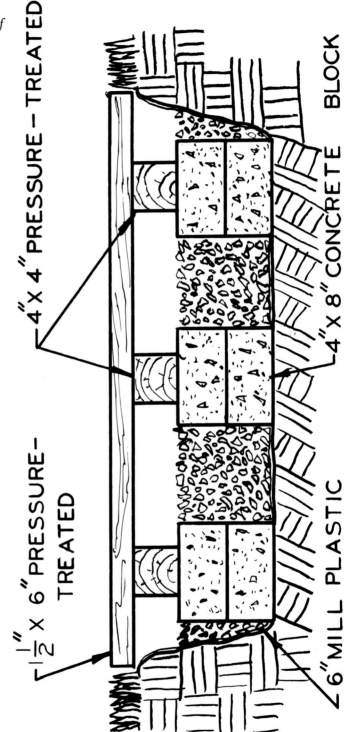

6 Small Projects

A number of small, simple projects using rough-sawn wood, weathered barn wood, and other rustic materials are presented here (Illus. 224–279, Color Illus. B7, B8). These projects require only basic construction techniques and are accompanied with detailed plans. I have also included photographs of products that incorporate innovative ideas, which you might want to consider in your own designs.

Illus. 224. Half-round shelf.

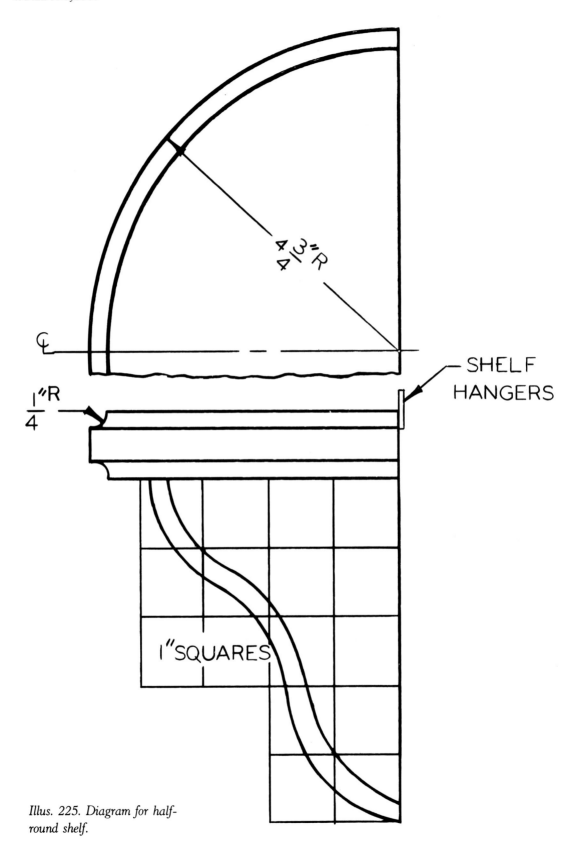

Illus. 225. Diagram for half-round shelf.

Illus. 226. Small rectangular shelf.

Illus. 227. Longer rectangular shelf with same basic details.

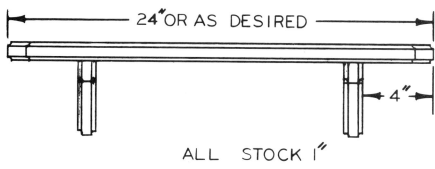

24" OR AS DESIRED

4"

ALL STOCK 1"

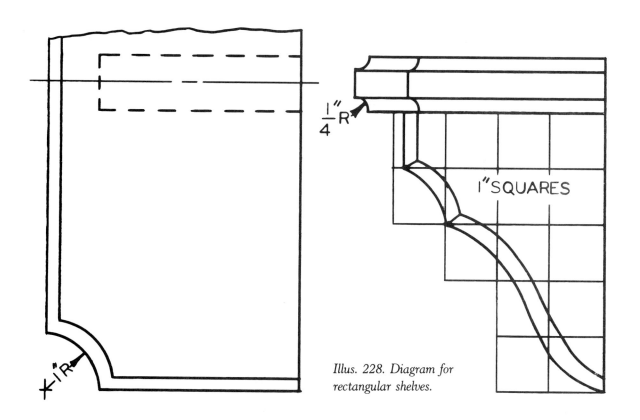

¼"R

¼"R

1"SQUARES

Illus. 228. Diagram for rectangular shelves.

Illus. 229. Another shelf design of heavier material.

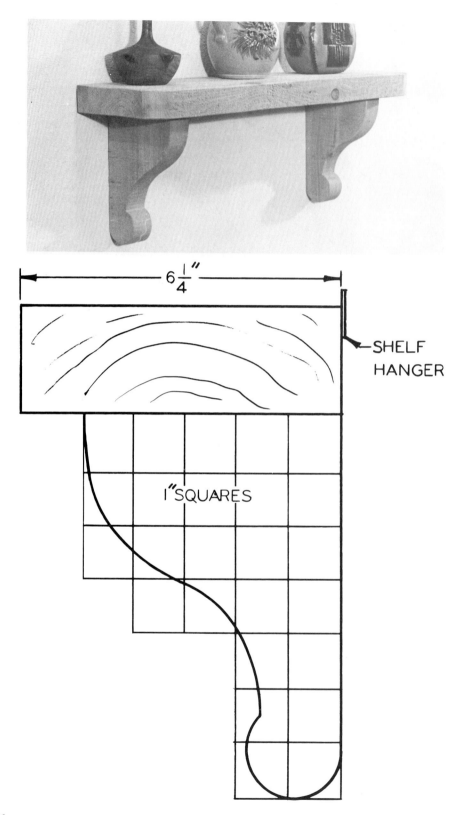

6 1/4"

SHELF
HANGER

1" SQUARES

Illus. 230. Diagram for shelf.

(Plans continued next page.)

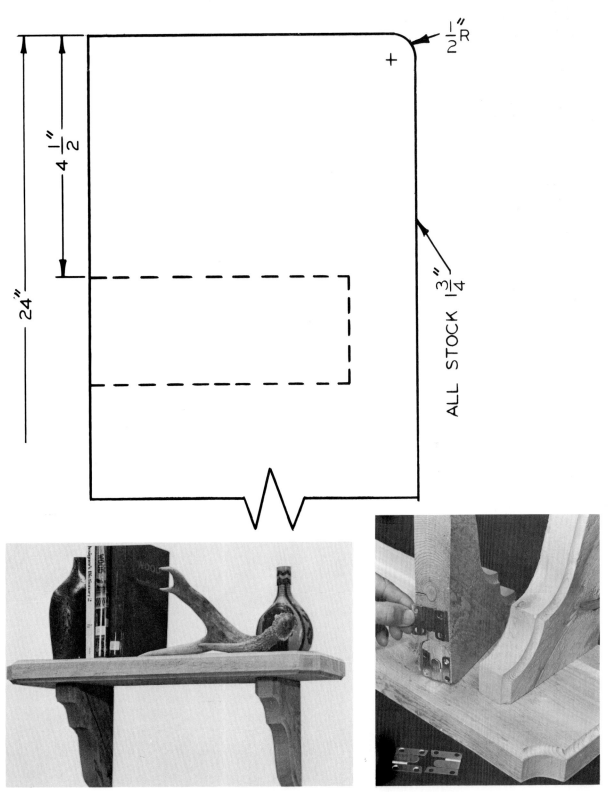

Illus. 231. Heavy-plank shelving with routed edges.

Illus. 232. Thick shelf brackets routed to accept flush-mount, interlocking connectors.

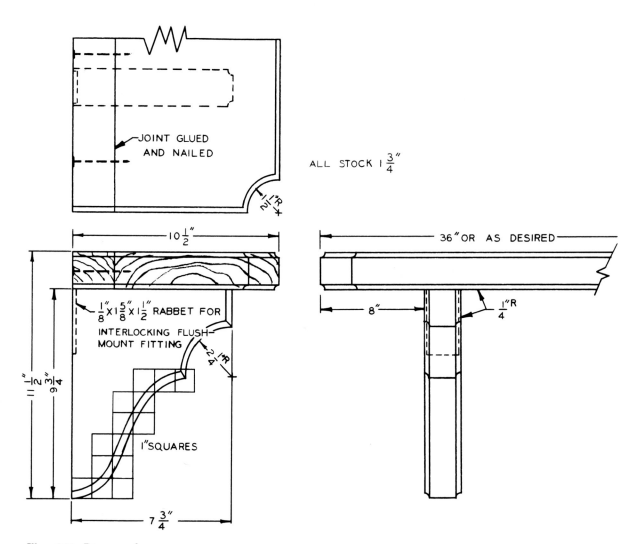

JOINT GLUED
AND NAILED

ALL STOCK 1 $\frac{3}{4}$ "

$\frac{1}{2}$ "R

10 $\frac{1}{2}$ "

$\frac{1}{8}$ " X 1 $\frac{5}{8}$ " X 1 $\frac{1}{2}$ " RABBET FOR
INTERLOCKING FLUSH-
MOUNT FITTING

2 $\frac{1}{4}$ "R

1"SQUARES

11 $\frac{1}{2}$ "
9 $\frac{3}{4}$ "

7 $\frac{3}{4}$ "

36" OR AS DESIRED

8"

$\frac{1}{4}$ "R

*Illus. 233. Diagram for
details of routed edge, plank
shelving.*

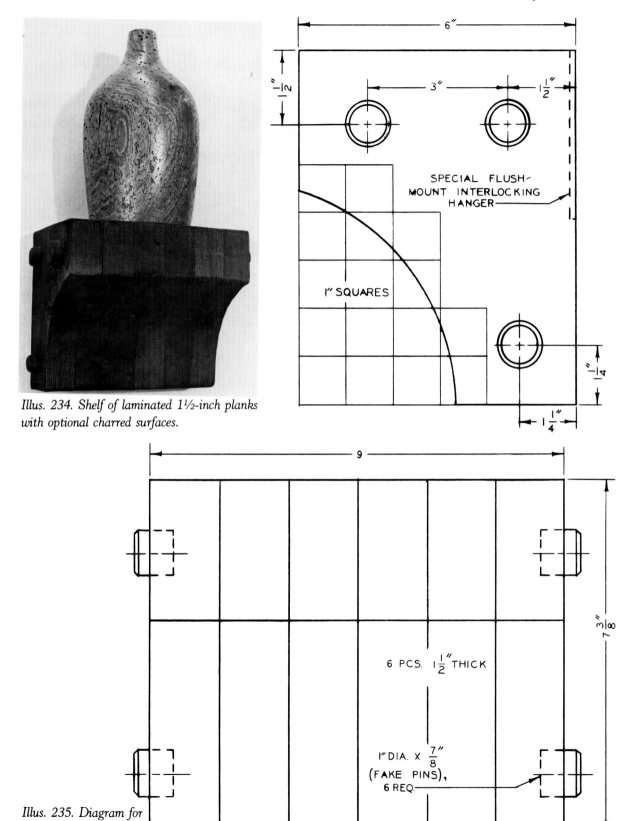

Illus. 234. *Shelf of laminated 1½-inch planks with optional charred surfaces.*

6″

1 1/2″

3″

1 1/2″

SPECIAL FLUSH-
MOUNT INTERLOCKING
HANGER

1″ SQUARES

1 1/4″

1 1/4″

9

7 3/8″

6 PCS. 1 1/2″ THICK

1″ DIA. X 7/8″
(FAKE PINS),
6 REQ.

Illus. 235. *Diagram for laminated plank shelf.*

Illus. 236. Snapshot holder.

*Illus. 237. A weathered-wood
snapshot holder.*

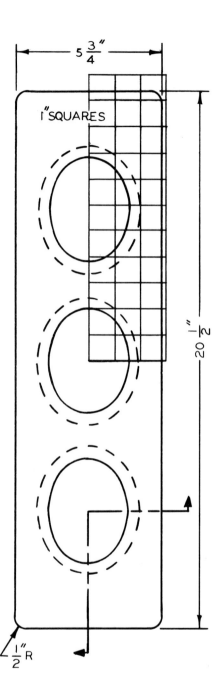

$5\frac{3}{4}''$

1"SQUARES

$20\frac{1}{2}''$

$\frac{1}{2}''$R

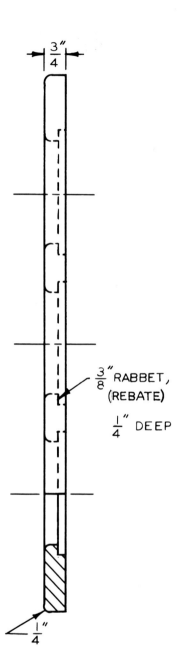

$\frac{3}{4}''$

$\frac{3}{8}''$ RABBET,
(REBATE)

$\frac{1}{4}''$ DEEP

$\frac{1}{4}''$

*Illus. 238. Diagram for three-
oval-hole frame. Note rabbet
router cut into back.*

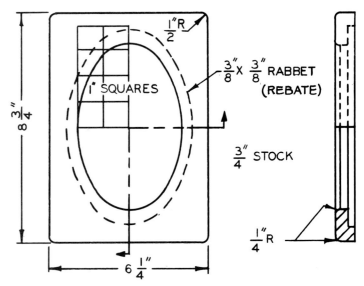

Illus. 239. Frame for an oval 5″ × 7″ photo.

Illus. 240. Diagram for 5″ × 7″ frame.

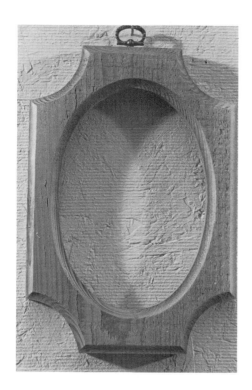

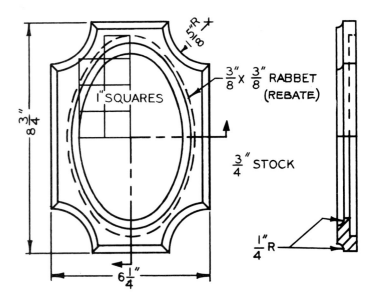

Illus. 241. Another rustic frame design for 5″ × 7″ photos.

Illus. 242. Diagram for oval picture frame. These designs can be enlarged for 8″ × 10″ photos.

*Illus. 243. An oval frame in
rustic barn wood.*

*Illus. 244. Another idea is
this "flat" frame set within
an "edge" frame, shown here
in barn wood.*

Illus. 245. Simple pegboard.

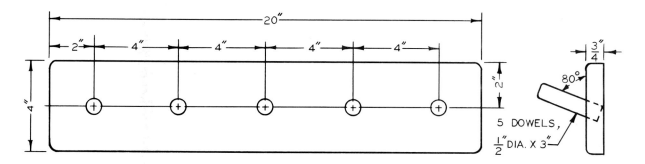

20″

2″ 4″ 4″ 4″ 4″

4″

2″

3/4″

80°

5 DOWELS,
1/2″ DIA. X 3″

Illus. 246. Diagram for pegboard.

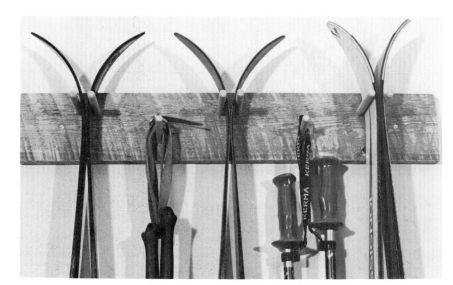

Illus. 247. Ski rack holds both cross-country and downhill skis.

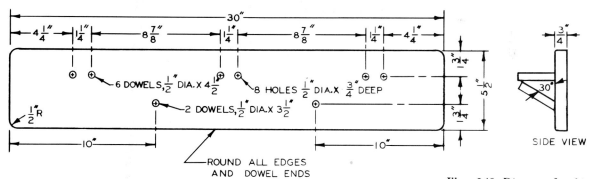

30″

4 1/4″ 1 1/4″ 8 7/8″ 1 1/4″ 8 7/8″ 1 1/4″ 4 1/4″

3/4″

3/4″

5 1/2″

3/4″

6 DOWELS, 1/2″ DIA. X 4 1/2″   8 HOLES 1/2″ DIA. X 3/4″ DEEP

1/2″ R

2 DOWELS, 1/2″ DIA. X 3 1/2″

10″   10″

ROUND ALL EDGES
AND DOWEL ENDS

3/4″

30°

SIDE VIEW

Illus. 248. Diagram for ski rack.

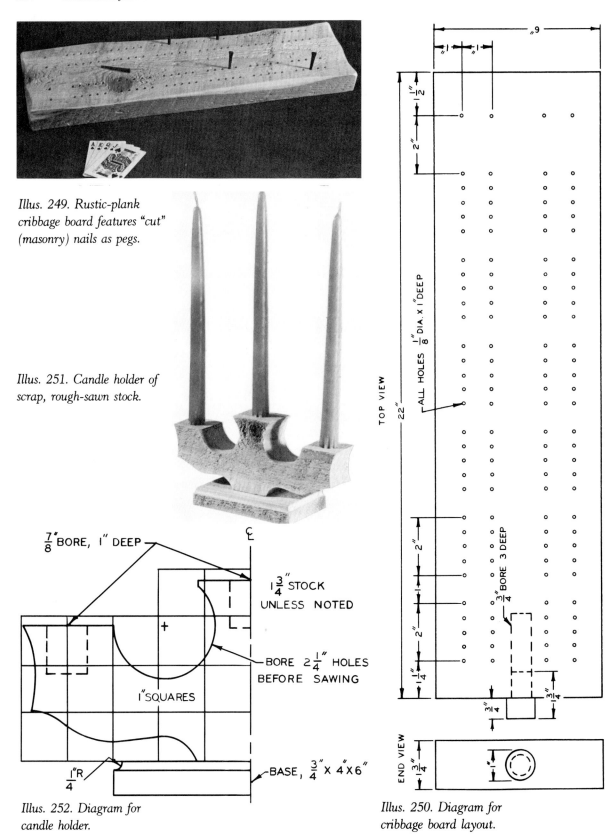

Illus. 249. Rustic-plank cribbage board features "cut" (masonry) nails as pegs.

Illus. 251. Candle holder of scrap, rough-sawn stock.

Illus. 252. Diagram for candle holder.

Illus. 250. Diagram for cribbage board layout.

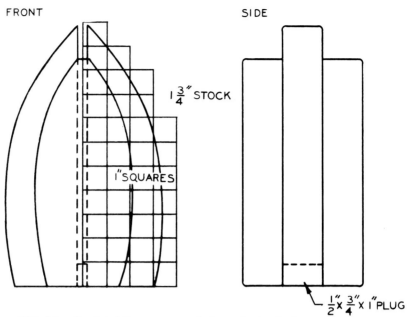

FRONT

SIDE

$1\frac{3}{4}''$ STOCK

1" SQUARES

$\frac{1}{2}'' \times \frac{3}{4}'' \times 1''$ PLUG

Illus. 253. Vase for dried flowers or weeds is made simply from plank cutouts.

Illus. 254. Diagram for rustic weed pot, Design I.

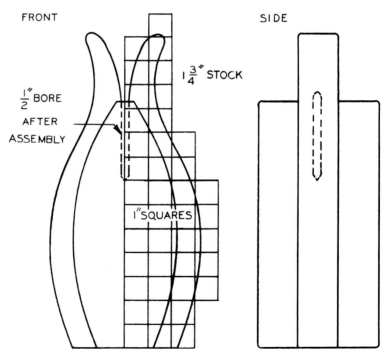

FRONT

SIDE

$\frac{1}{2}''$ BORE

AFTER

ASSEMBLY

$1\frac{3}{4}''$ STOCK

1" SQUARES

Illus. 255. Another plank-type weed pot. See page 135 for plant stand details.

Illus. 256. Drawing, weed pot, Design II.

Illus. 257. Slab clock is made with shotgun shell markers. Drawing was burned on by artist Christy Ohman.

Illus. 258. Texturing with a drum sander. To create an interesting edge texture, hold the sander in various positions and randomly apply the work.

Illus. 259. Another of Christy Ohman's artistic burnings on a slab of pine.

Illus. 260. A slab clock made with screw-hole plugs (buttons).

Illus. 261. A PEG-treated slab clock.

Illus. 262. Any old branch or post can be turned into an unusual lamp with these simple lines.

Illus. 263. A lathe-turned mug that has been surface-textured by a drum sander with a coarse abrasive. The surfaces were then sanded with a fine abrasive and stained to highlight the texturing. See Illus. 258.

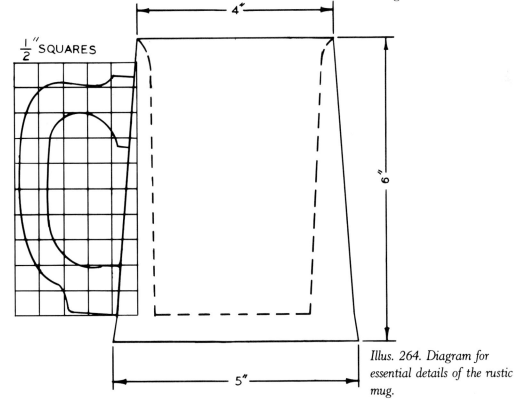

Illus. 264. Diagram for essential details of the rustic mug.

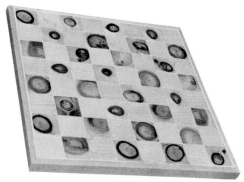

Illus. 265. Alternating clear and knot mosaics make this unusual board for chess and checkers.

Illus. 266. Box top of thin, knot mosaics.

Illus. 267. Bird feeder with small, tapered, sawn shingles.

TOP VIEW

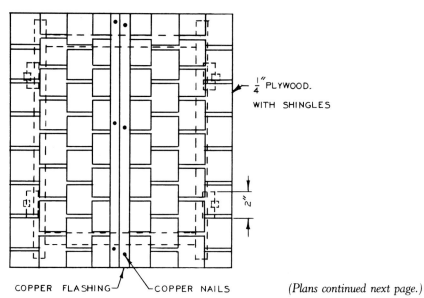

¼" PLYWOOD.
WITH SHINGLES

2"

COPPER FLASHING

COPPER NAILS

Illus. 268. Diagram for bird feeder.

(Plans continued next page.)

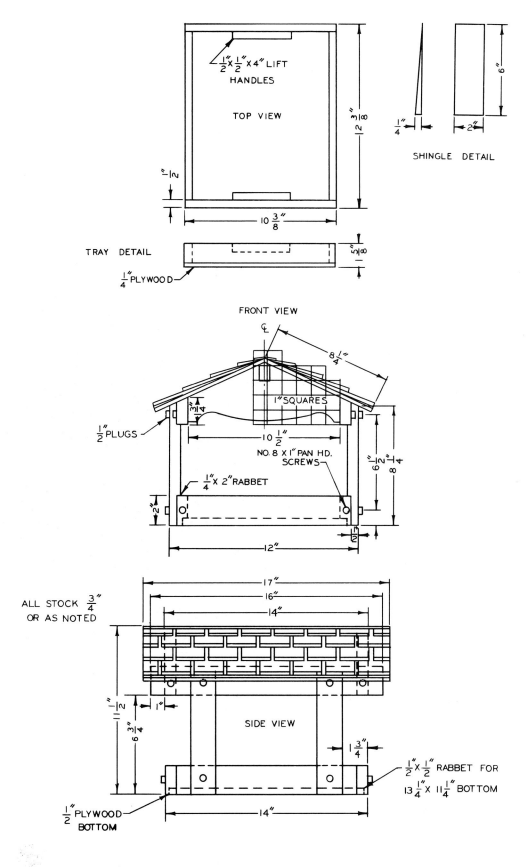

$\frac{1}{2}" \times \frac{1}{2}" \times 4"$ LIFT HANDLES

TOP VIEW

$12\frac{3}{8}"$

$\frac{1}{2}"$

$10\frac{3}{8}"$

SHINGLE DETAIL

$\frac{1}{4}"$

$2"$

$6"$

TRAY DETAIL

$\frac{5}{8}"$

$\frac{1}{4}"$ PLYWOOD

FRONT VIEW

₵

$8\frac{1}{4}"$

$\frac{3}{4}"$

1" SQUARES

$\frac{1}{2}"$ PLUGS

$10\frac{1}{2}"$

NO. 8 X 1" PAN HD. SCREWS

$\frac{1}{4}" \times 2"$ RABBET

$6\frac{1}{2}"$

$8\frac{1}{4}"$

$2"$

$\frac{1}{2}"$

$12"$

ALL STOCK $\frac{3}{4}"$ OR AS NOTED

$17"$

$16"$

$14"$

$1\frac{1}{2}"$

$1"$

$6\frac{3}{4}"$

SIDE VIEW

$1\frac{3}{4}"$

$\frac{1}{2}" \times \frac{1}{2}"$ RABBET FOR $13\frac{1}{4}" \times 11\frac{1}{4}"$ BOTTOM

$\frac{1}{2}"$ PLYWOOD BOTTOM

$14"$

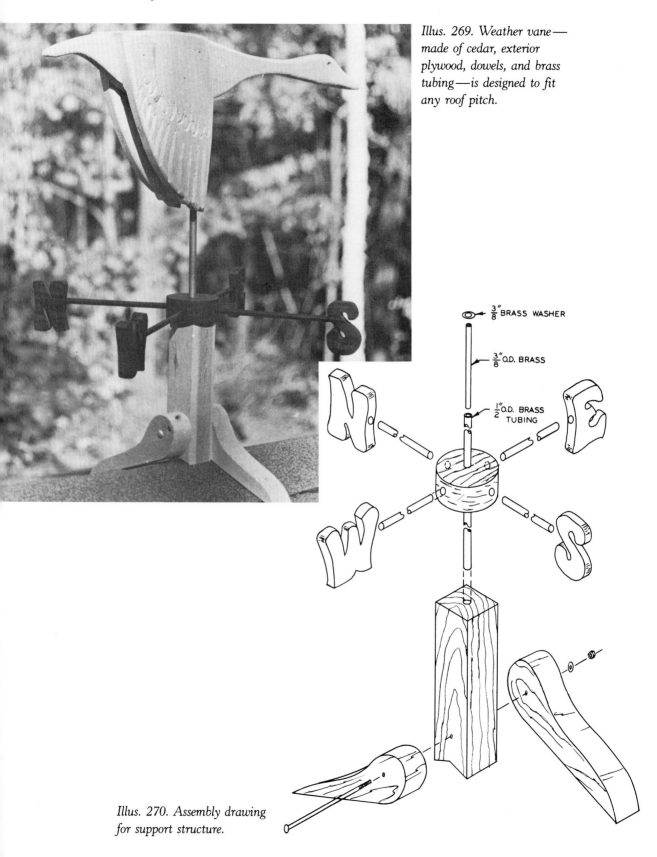

Illus. 269. Weather vane—made of cedar, exterior plywood, dowels, and brass tubing—is designed to fit any roof pitch.

⅜" BRASS WASHER

⅜" O.D. BRASS

½" O.D. BRASS TUBING

Illus. 270. Assembly drawing for support structure.

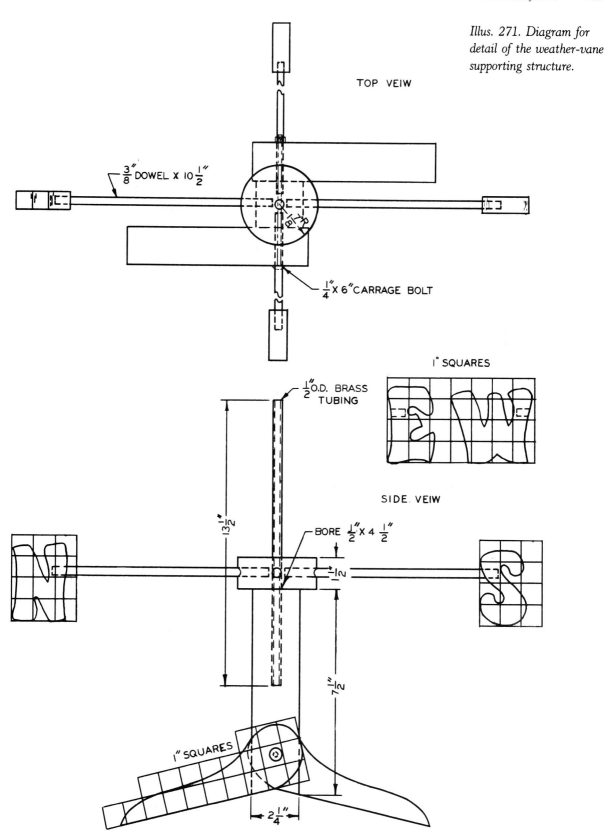

Illus. 271. Diagram for detail of the weather-vane supporting structure.

TOP VEIW

$\frac{3}{8}$" DOWEL X 10$\frac{1}{2}$"

$\frac{1}{4}$" X 6" CARRAGE BOLT

1" SQUARES

$\frac{1}{2}$" O.D. BRASS TUBING

SIDE VEIW

13$\frac{1}{2}$"

BORE $\frac{1}{2}$" X 4 $\frac{1}{2}$"

$\frac{1}{2}$"

7$\frac{1}{2}$"

1" SQUARES

2$\frac{1}{4}$"

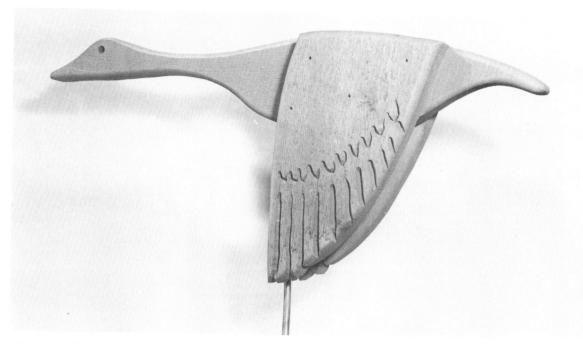

*Illus. 272. Flying goose
weather vane.*

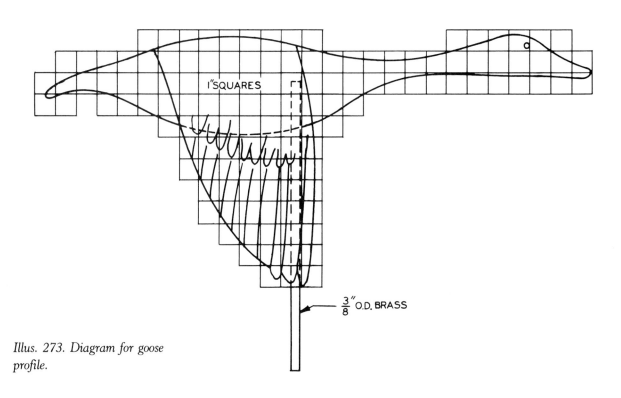

I"SQUARES

a

$\frac{3}{8}$" O.D. BRASS

*Illus. 273. Diagram for goose
profile.*

Illus. 274. Serpent weather vane.

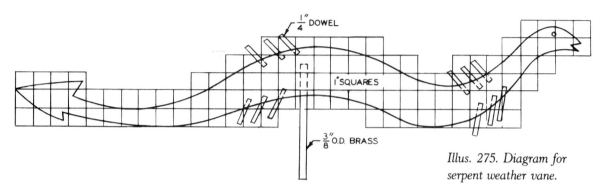

Illus. 275. Diagram for serpent weather vane.

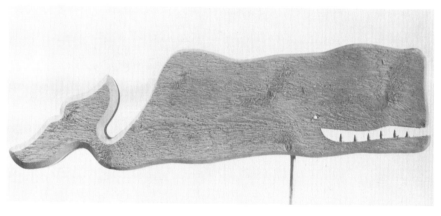

Illus. 276. Whale weather vane.

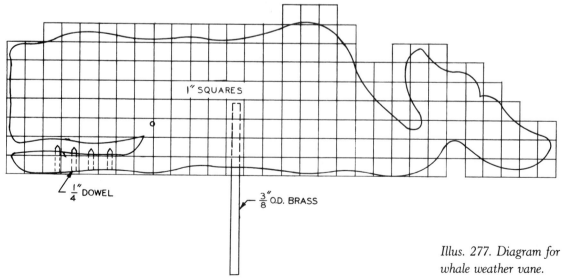

Illus. 277. Diagram for whale weather vane.

Illus. 278. Rooster weather vane.

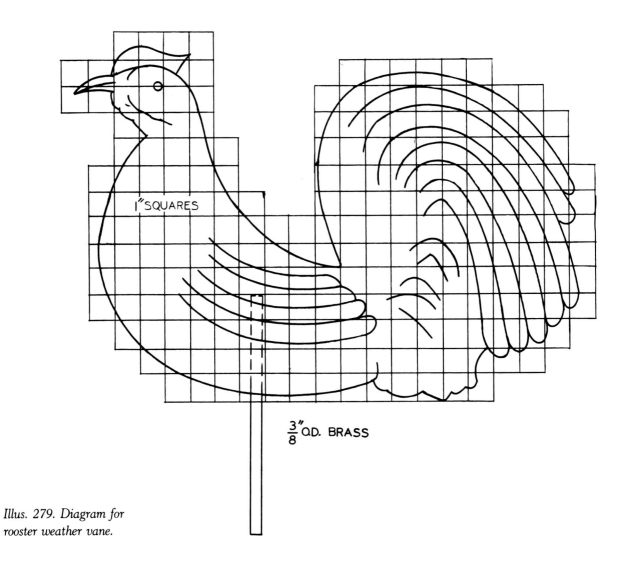

1"SQUARES

$\frac{3}{8}$" O.D. BRASS

Illus. 279. Diagram for rooster weather vane.

7 Wooden Mailboxes

The wooden mailbox is especially significant for woodworkers, because it symbolizes the craft. This chapter illustrates the Wood Works' popular, rural mailbox (Illus. 280–281), our matching posts, and also some urban (wall-mounted) mailboxes.

We designed the wooden, country mailbox to replace old, battered and rusty metal boxes and cheap, plastic ones that mar the scenery of country roads and suburban developments. We manufacture these rural mailboxes in rustic cedar (Illus. 282) and in a smooth redwood version too.

Since our rural mailbox design has become so popular, we have released plans to home woodworkers so that they can make one for themselves. The plans are actually sold as a Plan Kit and include the following: complete drawings; illustrated assembly instructions; our custom-made, textured, UV-stabilized, exterior-brand plastic for making the straps and flag parts; and plans and mounting details for our standard post (see Illus. 285). With the exception of our special weatherproof plastic that simulates metal and never needs painting, all other materials are available from any lumberyard or hardware dealer.

For woodworkers who want it all packaged, we offer a Parts Kit (Illus. 283), which includes a metal liner, screws, marine-grade glue, and premachined pieces of rustic cedar (redwood is available by special order). You need only a ruler, screwdriver, and hammer to assemble the mailbox. You don't need special clamps. Detailed and illustrated instructions make assembly easy. We will even personalize it for you at a modest charge. All pieces and the routed, personalized, surfaces are unfinished (not stained or painted). Choose from several post designs (Illus. 284–291, Color Illus. B10), all of which can be used in combination with the rural, wooden mailbox. Refer to page 159 for information about ordering rural mailboxes, Plan Kits, Parts Kits and posts or Post Plans.

Four designs for urban, wall-mounted mailboxes are also included in this chapter. The first three (Illus. 292–298) are similar in appearance and construction; they have identical covers, but the fronts differ in order to accommodate router-carved names or numbers. Refer to my earlier book *Making Wood Signs* (Sterling Publishing Co., 1981) for information about carving names and numbers on your mailbox.

The final project in this chapter is another urban, wall-mounted mailbox that differs greatly from the others. It has small shingles stapled and glued (with marine-quality adhesive) to ⅜-inch and ¼-inch (cover) exterior plywood (Illus. 299–300). Refer to page 72 for shingle-making techniques.

Illus. 280. *This trademarked sticker is affixed to the inside of every mailbox and Parts Kit.*

Illus. 281. *The appealing rustic cedar mailbox can be personalized with a router.*

Illus. 282. *Spielmans' mailboxes are made of 1″ decay-free cedar that's built over a U.S. Postal Service–approved metal liner. Exterior parts are noncorrosive and age beautifully.*

Illus. 283. *Spielmans' Parts Kit contains all necessary premachined parts, a metal liner, glue, and illustrated, easy, step-by-step instructions.*

Illus. 284. A simple,
4″ × 4″ cedar post.

Illus. 285. Our standard post
is the most popular. The
planter base (plan on page
137) is an optional idea. A
square hole cut in the bottom
lets the post slip through the
planter for in-the-ground
anchoring. Otherwise, cut off
the post and fill the planter
with dirt or stones to make a
portable unit.

Illus. 286. This post with
paper tube eliminates those
ugly, brightly painted (or
rusted) metal tubes that hold
newspapers. Refer to page
159 to order plans.

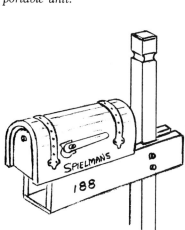

Illus. 287. Another
newspaper-holder design is
this boxed arm post. See
page 159 to order plans.

Illus. 288. The dovetail
arm post is rustic-looking
and solidly built. See page
159.

Illus. 289. A bird or animal
can be cut into the post top
or carved, then attached to it.

Illus. 290. This combination sign and wood mailbox makes a pleasing introduction for any home.

Illus. 291. A large-scale tusk mortise-and-tenon joint makes this style post easy to disassemble, which is ideal for seasonal usage and for transportation purposes.

Illus. 292. The most popular city mailbox at the Wood Works.

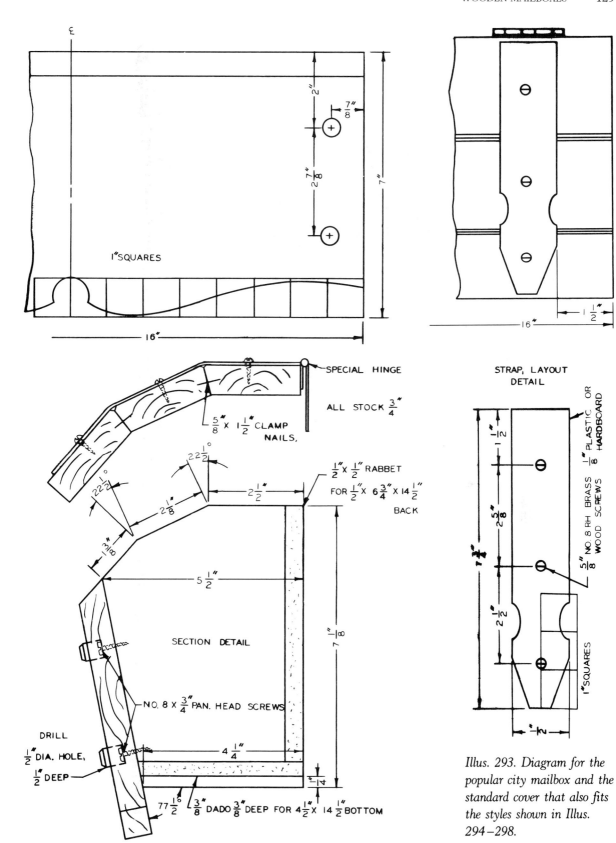

1" SQUARES

SPECIAL HINGE

ALL STOCK $\frac{3}{4}$"

$\frac{5}{8}$" X 1 $\frac{1}{2}$" CLAMP NAILS,

$\frac{1}{2}$" X $\frac{1}{2}$" RABBET

FOR $\frac{1}{2}$" X 6 $\frac{3}{4}$" X 14 $\frac{1}{2}$"

BACK

SECTION DETAIL

NO. 8 X $\frac{3}{4}$" PAN. HEAD SCREWS

DRILL

$\frac{1}{2}$" DIA. HOLE,

$\frac{1}{2}$" DEEP

$\frac{3}{8}$" DADO $\frac{3}{8}$" DEEP FOR 4 $\frac{1}{2}$" X 14 $\frac{1}{2}$" BOTTOM

STRAP, LAYOUT DETAIL

$\frac{1}{8}$" PLASTIC OR HARDBOARD

$\frac{5}{8}$" NO. 8 RH BRASS WOOD SCREWS

1" SQUARES

Illus. 293. Diagram for the popular city mailbox and the standard cover that also fits the styles shown in Illus. 294–298.

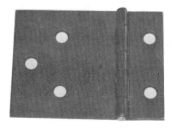

Illus. 294. Hinge with unequal leaves is used for all three wooden city mailboxes of similar design.

Illus. 295. Another style of wall-mounted mailbox that uses the exact same cover.

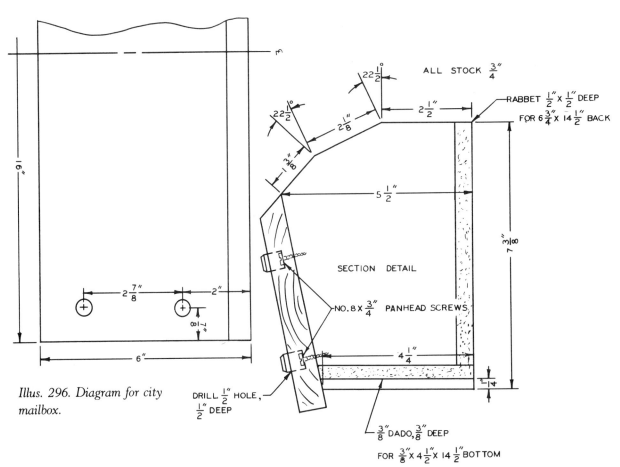

Illus. 296. Diagram for city mailbox.

Illus. 297. *The third of three different but similar mailbox designs.*

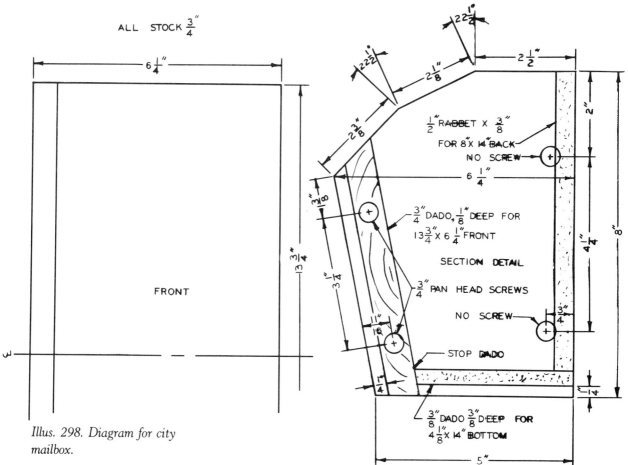

ALL STOCK $\frac{3}{4}''$

$6\frac{1}{4}''$

$13\frac{3}{4}''$

FRONT

3

Illus. 298. *Diagram for city mailbox.*

$22\frac{1}{2}°$

$22\frac{1}{2}°$

$2\frac{1}{8}''$

$22\frac{1}{2}°$

$2\frac{3}{4}''$

$2\frac{1}{2}''$

2"

$\frac{1}{2}''$ RABBET X $\frac{3}{8}''$
FOR 8" X 14" BACK
NO SCREW

$6\frac{1}{4}''$

$\frac{3}{4}''$ DADO, $\frac{1}{8}''$ DEEP FOR
$13\frac{3}{4}''$ X $6\frac{1}{4}''$ FRONT

SECTION DETAIL

$\frac{3}{8}''$

$\frac{3}{4}''$ PAN HEAD SCREWS

NO SCREW

$\frac{3}{4}''$

$4\frac{1}{4}''$

8"

$3\frac{1}{4}''$

$\frac{1}{16}''$

$\frac{1}{4}''$

STOP DADO

$1\frac{1}{4}''$

$\frac{3}{8}''$ DADO $\frac{3}{8}''$ DEEP FOR
$4\frac{1}{8}''$ X 14" BOTTOM

5"

Illus. 299. A shingled city (wall-mounted) mailbox.

FRONT VIEW   SIDE VIEW

SHINGLE DETAIL

$\frac{1}{4}$"PLYWOOD, $5\frac{3}{4}$" X 11"

SMALL STRAP HINGE

INNER BOX, $\frac{3}{8}$"
PLYWOOD WITH
BUTT JOINTS

6"

2"

9"

$8\frac{3}{4}$"

$9\frac{3}{4}$"

$4\frac{1}{2}$"

$1\frac{1}{4}$"

Illus. 300. Diagram for shingled mailbox.

8 Indoor and Outdoor Furniture

Plant stands, planters, a gun cabinet, firewood boxes, a bar, a number of easy-to-make coffee or end tables, various round tables and stools, and practically our entire line of current furniture designs are illustrated in this chapter (Illus. 301–369, Color Illus. C11–14, D15–19). Detailed plans accompany most of the projects, except the trestle tables, some of the benches, and the swing sets. Plans for these items can be ordered directly as indicated on page 159.

Depending upon the kind or, more specifically, the size of material available, you may have to modify certain plans. For example, if the plan specifies 1¾-inch-thick wood, and you have 1½-inch-thick wood, convert certain details accordingly. In most cases, using thinner stock than specified should not pose any particular problem other than an insignificant change in appearance. Strength or structural performance will be relatively unchanged. Be sure to use decay-resistant woods, such as cedar, redwood, cypress, or a pressure-treated wood, for outdoor projects—particularly those that will be in contact with the ground. Waterproof glue should, obviously, be used for outdoor projects. Also, conceal all metal fasteners where possible under plugs or pegs to prevent unsightly rust or staining of the surrounding surfaces. Suitable nontoxic sealers, water repellents, and other optional finishes are described in chapter 4.

Illus. 301. Simple plant stands.

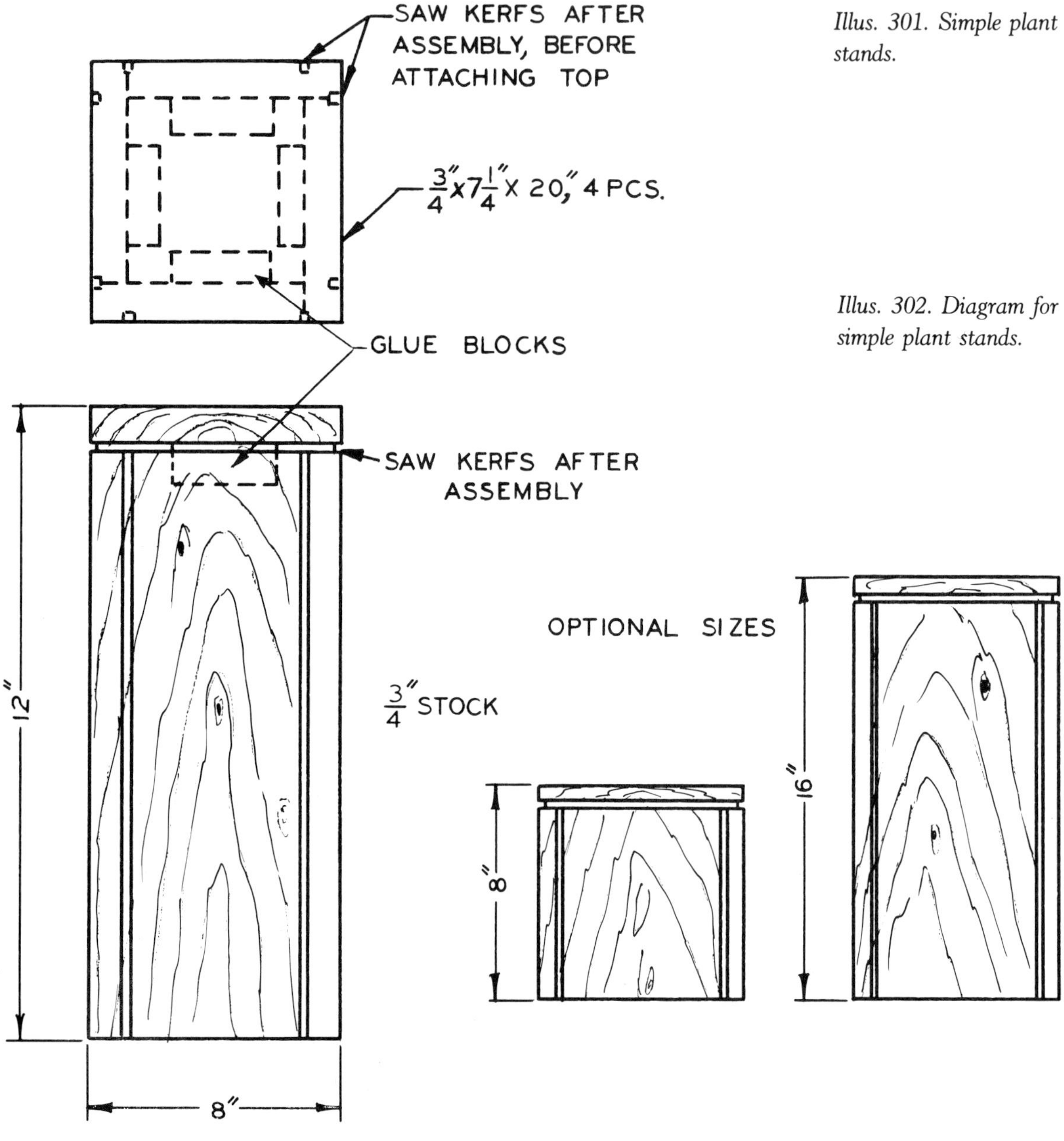

SAW KERFS AFTER ASSEMBLY, BEFORE ATTACHING TOP

$\frac{3}{4}"x7\frac{1}{4}"X 20,"$ 4 PCS.

Illus. 302. Diagram for simple plant stands.

GLUE BLOCKS

SAW KERFS AFTER ASSEMBLY

OPTIONAL SIZES

$\frac{3}{4}"$ STOCK

12"

8"

8"

16"

Illus. 303. Shingled plant stands.

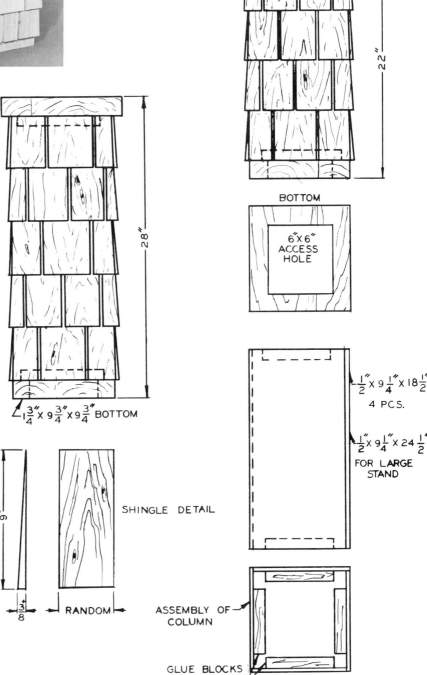

$1\frac{3}{4}" \times 11\frac{1}{2}" \times 11\frac{1}{2}"$ TOP

22"

BOTTOM

$6" \times 6"$ ACCESS HOLE

$1\frac{3}{4}" \times 9\frac{3}{4}" \times 9\frac{3}{4}"$ BOTTOM

28"

9"

$\frac{3}{8}$

RANDOM

SHINGLE DETAIL

$\frac{1}{2}" \times 9\frac{1}{4}" \times 18\frac{1}{2}"$
4 PCS.

$\frac{1}{2}" \times 9\frac{1}{4}" \times 24\frac{1}{2}"$
FOR LARGE STAND

ASSEMBLY OF COLUMN

GLUE BLOCKS

Illus. 304. Diagram for shingled plant stands.

Illus. 305. Octagon plank planters.

Illus. 306. Planters can be made in various sizes.

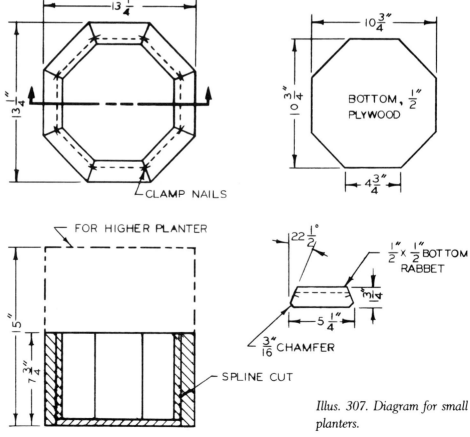

Illus. 307. Diagram for small planters.

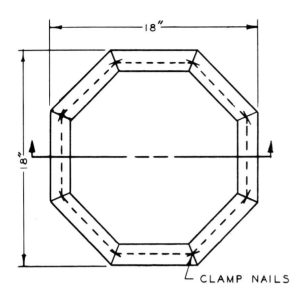

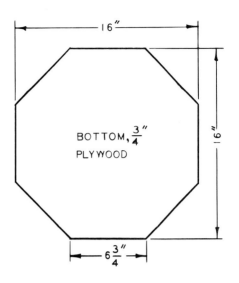

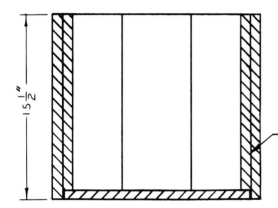

CLAMP NAILS

SPLINE CUT

Illus. 308. Diagram for large planter.

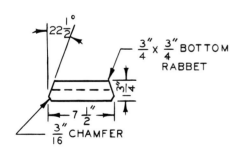

22 $\frac{1}{2}$°

$\frac{3}{4}$" × $\frac{3}{4}$" BOTTOM RABBET

$\frac{3}{4}$"

7 $\frac{1}{2}$"

$\frac{3}{16}$" CHAMFER

Illus. 309. Rustic gun cabinet is made from 1- and 2-inch rough-sawn material. Back of interior is shingled.

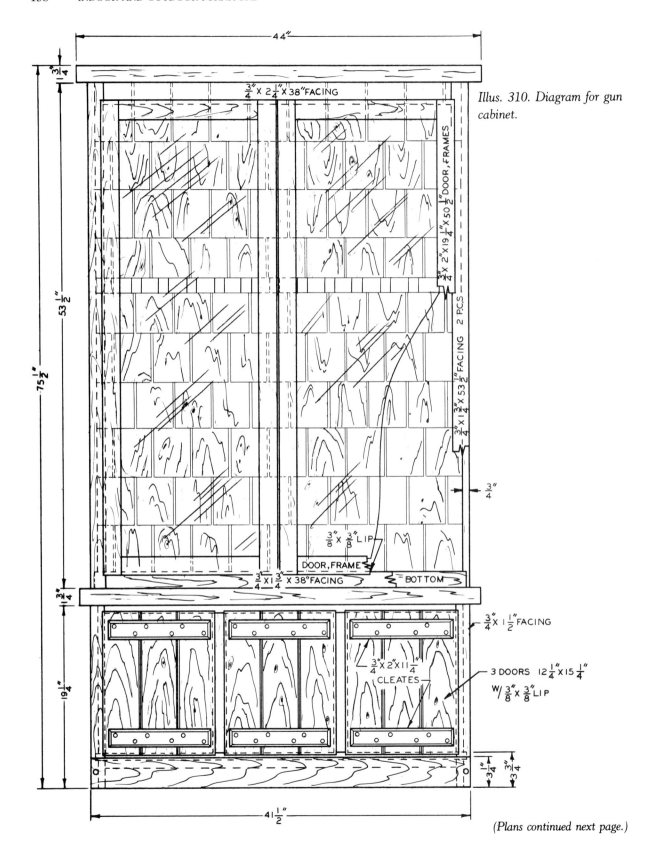

Illus. 310. Diagram for gun cabinet.

(Plans continued next page.)

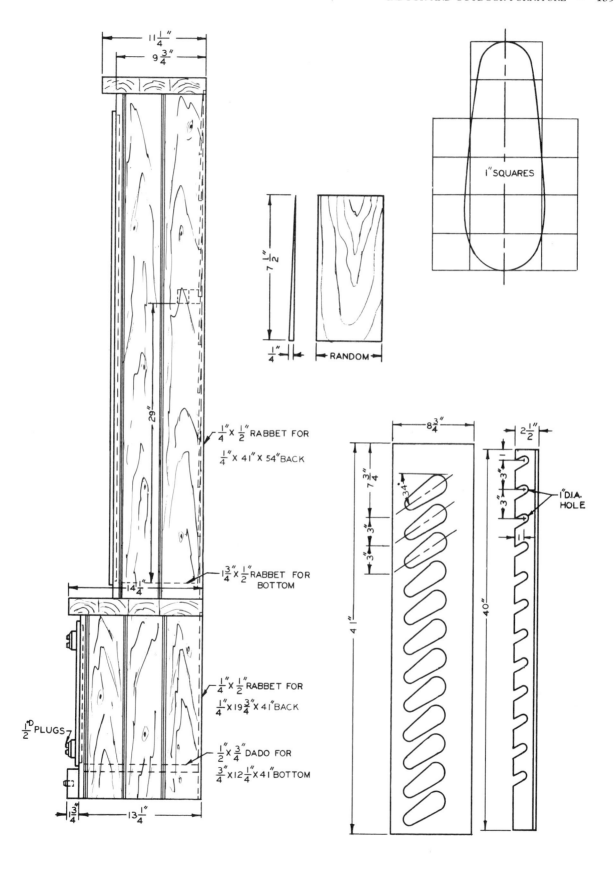

11 1/4"

9 3/4"

7 1/2"

1/4"

RANDOM

1" SQUARES

29"

1/4" X 1/2" RABBET FOR
1/4" X 41" X 54" BACK

1 3/4" X 1/2" RABBET FOR
BOTTOM

14 1/4"

1/4" X 1/2" RABBET FOR
1/4" X 19 3/4" X 41" BACK

1/2" PLUGS

1/2" X 3/4" DADO FOR
3/4" X 12 1/4" X 41" BOTTOM

3/4"

13 1/4"

8 3/4"

7 3/4"

3/4"

3"

3"

3"

2 1/2"

3"

3"

1" D.I.A.
HOLE

41"

40"

Illus. 311. The butts of the guns rest inside routed-out recesses.

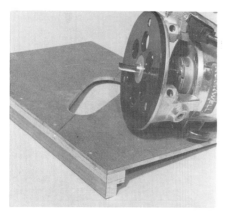

Illus. 312. To make identical recesses, use a special template and a template guide on the router base.

Illus. 313. A closeup look at the bit protruding through the template guide.

TOP VIEW

END VIEW

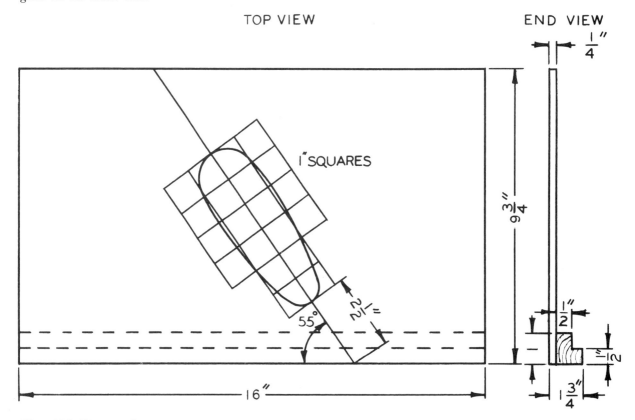

1" SQUARES

Illus. 314. Diagram for template.

Illus. 316. Cuts are recessed so guns tip towards rear of cabinet.

Illus. 315. The template setup for routing.

Illus. 318. Detail of upper cabinet side with facing attached.

Illus. 317. Upper section is shown without doors.

(Below left) Illus. 320. Using glue and staples to secure the shingles.

(Below right) Illus. 321. Attaching the final row with hot-melt adhesive so no nails or staples show.

Illus. 319. Shingling over the ¼-inch plywood back.

Illus. 322. Use simple, glued lap joints for the door frames.

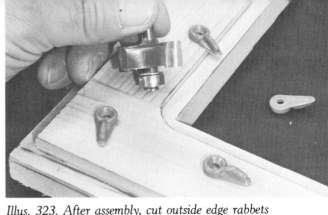

Illus. 323. After assembly, cut outside edge rabbets (3/8" × 3/8") for lip and hinges. (See Illus. 326.) Rout inside for glass as shown. Chisel corners square. Notice retainers that hold recessed glass.

Illus. 324. Front view of lower cabinet. Note cabinet facing, particle board (which is a board made from resin-bonded wooden pieces) bottom and plywood back.

Illus. 325. Rear view of same cabinet. Note glue blocks. The back extends 1/2 inch above sides so it can be rabbeted into the top.

(Left) Illus. 326. Attach 3/8" × 3/8" lip and offset hinges to the glass doors in the upper cabinet and to these solid doors of the lower cabinet.

(Above) Illus. 327. The completed lower cabinet ready for optional door locks.

Illus 328. This firewood box was made from old, painted, used barn wood.

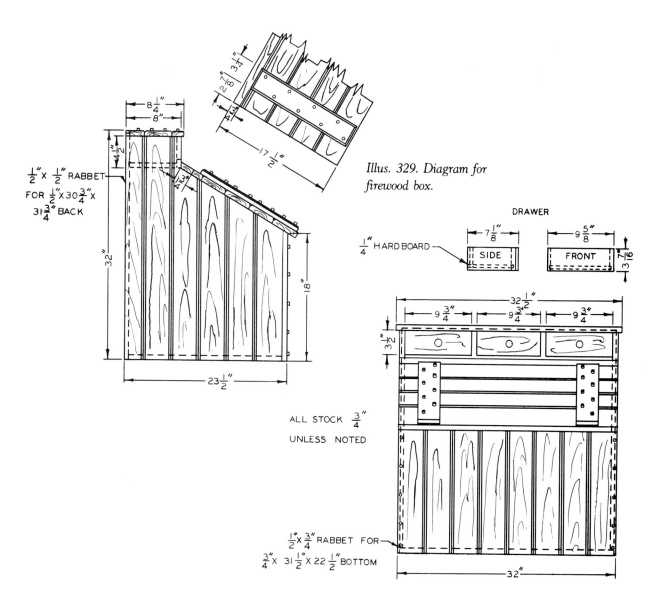

Illus. 329. Diagram for firewood box.

8 1/4"
8"

4 1/2"

1/2" x 1/2" RABBET
FOR 1/2" X 30 3/4" X
31 3/4" BACK

32"

18"

23 1/2"

2 7/8" 3 1/4"

3/4

17 1/2"

3/4

ALL STOCK 3/4"
UNLESS NOTED

DRAWER

1/4" HARDBOARD

7 1/8"
SIDE

9 5/8"
FRONT

3 7/16"

32 1/2"

9 3/4"   9 3/4"   9 3/4"

3 1/2"

1/2" X 3/4" RABBET FOR
3/4" X 31 1/2" X 22 1/2" BOTTOM

32"

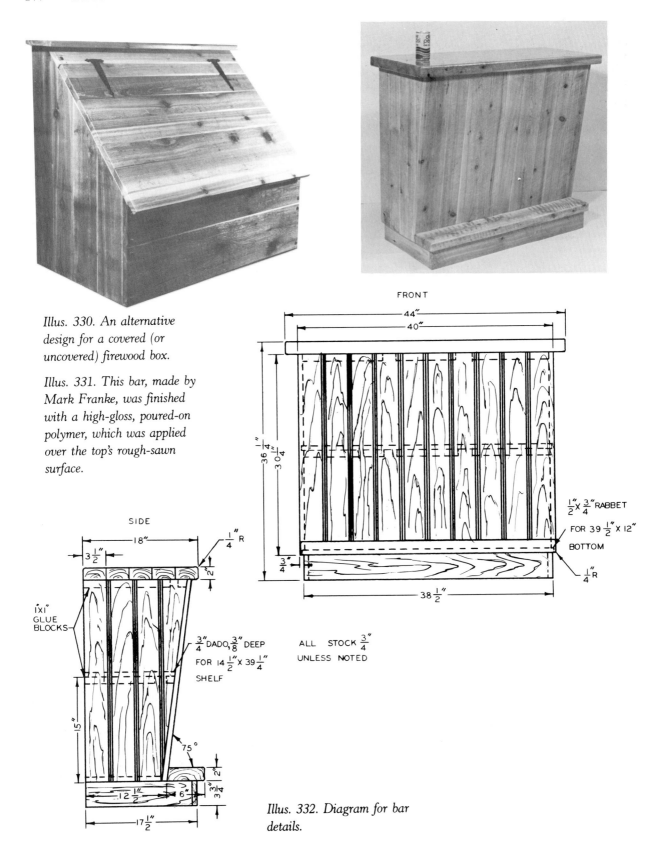

Illus. 330. An alternative design for a covered (or uncovered) firewood box.

Illus. 331. This bar, made by Mark Franke, was finished with a high-gloss, poured-on polymer, which was applied over the top's rough-sawn surface.

FRONT

$\frac{1}{2}$"X $\frac{3}{4}$"RABBET

FOR 39 $\frac{1}{2}$" X 12"

BOTTOM

$\frac{1}{4}$"R

SIDE

$\frac{1}{4}$"R

1"X1"
GLUE
BLOCKS

$\frac{3}{4}$"DADO, $\frac{3}{8}$" DEEP

FOR 14 $\frac{1}{2}$" X 39 $\frac{1}{4}$"

SHELF

ALL STOCK $\frac{3}{4}$"
UNLESS NOTED

75°

Illus. 332. Diagram for bar details.

Illus. 333. 2 × 4's, dowels, and glass are easily combined to make this coffee table.

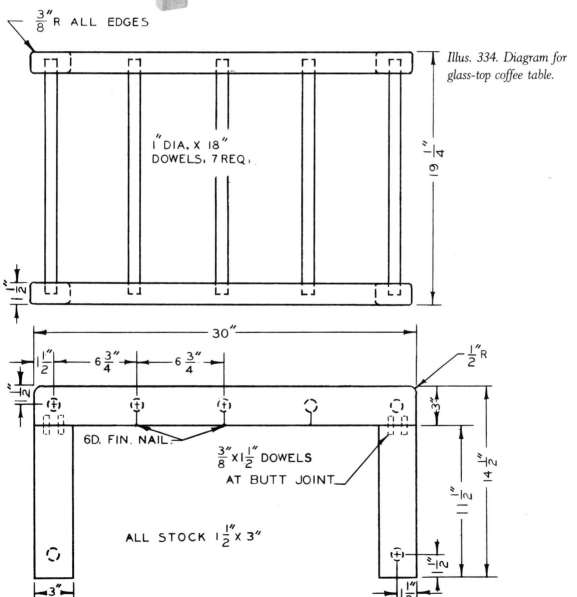

$\frac{3}{8}$" R ALL EDGES

Illus. 334. Diagram for glass-top coffee table.

1" DIA. X 18" DOWELS, 7 REQ,

$19 \frac{1}{4}$"

$\frac{1}{2}$"

30"

$1\frac{1}{2}$"

$6 \frac{3}{4}$" $6 \frac{3}{4}$"

$\frac{1}{2}$" R

3"

$\frac{1}{2}$"

6D. FIN. NAIL

$\frac{3}{8}$" X $1\frac{1}{2}$" DOWELS AT BUTT JOINT

$14 \frac{1}{2}$"

$1\frac{1}{2}$"

ALL STOCK $1\frac{1}{2}$" X 3"

3"

$\frac{1}{2}$"

$1\frac{1}{2}$"

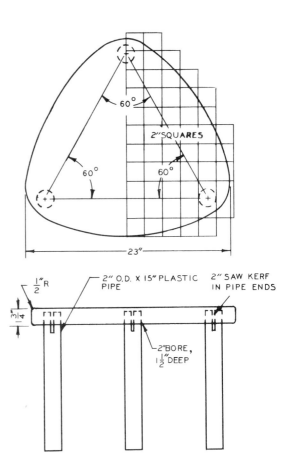

Illus. 335. Three-legged table with standard plastic pipe for legs. It disassembles easily for storage or transportation.

Illus. 336. Diagram for three-legged table.

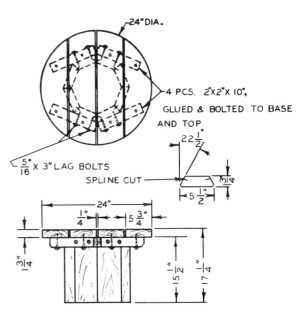

Illus. 337. Small, round, plank-top tables are useful indoors or out. Select 2-, 2½-, or 3-foot diameter.

Illus. 338. Diagram. 2-foot-diameter table.

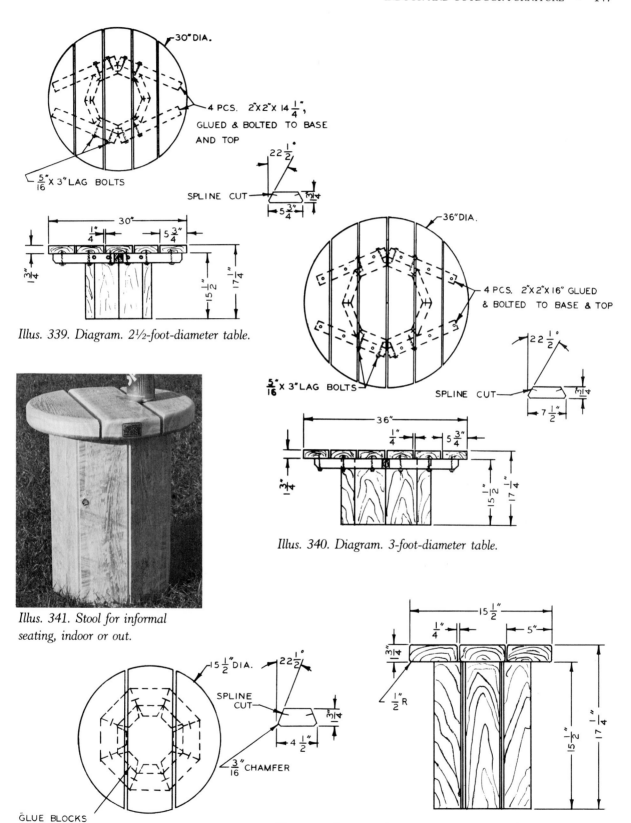

30" DIA.

4 PCS. 2"X 2"X 14$\frac{1}{4}$",
GLUED & BOLTED TO BASE
AND TOP

$\frac{5}{16}$"X 3" LAG BOLTS

22$\frac{1}{2}$°

SPLINE CUT

5$\frac{3}{4}$"

3$\frac{1}{4}$"

30"

$\frac{1}{4}$"

5$\frac{3}{4}$"

3$\frac{1}{4}$"

15$\frac{1}{2}$"

17$\frac{1}{4}$"

Illus. 339. Diagram. 2½-foot-diameter table.

36" DIA.

4 PCS. 2"X 2"X 16" GLUED
& BOLTED TO BASE & TOP

$\frac{5}{16}$"X 3" LAG BOLTS

22$\frac{1}{2}$°

SPLINE CUT

7$\frac{1}{2}$"

3$\frac{1}{4}$"

36"

$\frac{1}{4}$"

5$\frac{3}{4}$"

3$\frac{1}{4}$"

15$\frac{1}{2}$"

17$\frac{1}{4}$"

Illus. 340. Diagram. 3-foot-diameter table.

*Illus. 341. Stool for informal
seating, indoor or out.*

15$\frac{1}{2}$" DIA.

SPLINE
CUT

22$\frac{1}{2}$°

3$\frac{1}{4}$"

4$\frac{1}{2}$"

$\frac{3}{16}$" CHAMFER

GLUE BLOCKS
HOLD TOP & BASE

15$\frac{1}{2}$"

$\frac{1}{4}$"

5"

3$\frac{1}{4}$"

$\frac{1}{2}$" R

15$\frac{1}{2}$"

17$\frac{1}{4}$"

Illus. 342. Diagram for stool.

Illus. 343. This large, 4-foot- diameter table with stools makes a nice picnic set.

Illus. 344. Same style set, but edges of seat- and table-top planks have been rounded over.

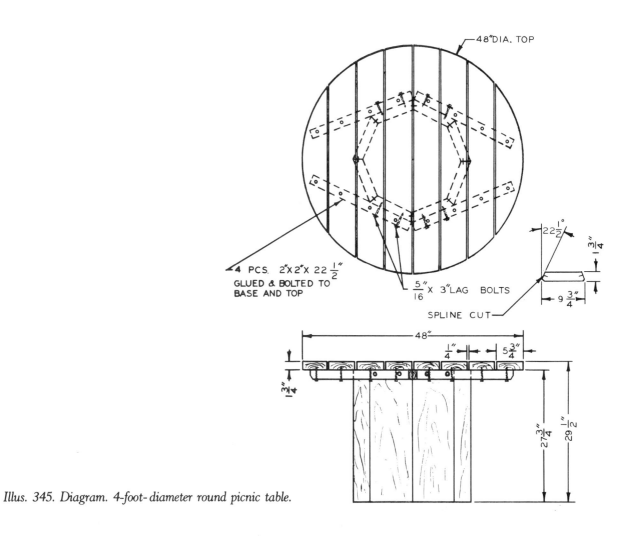

Illus. 345. Diagram. 4-foot- diameter round picnic table.

Illus. 346. 4-foot round picnic table with curved trestle benches.

Illus. 347. A closer look at the curved trestle bench.

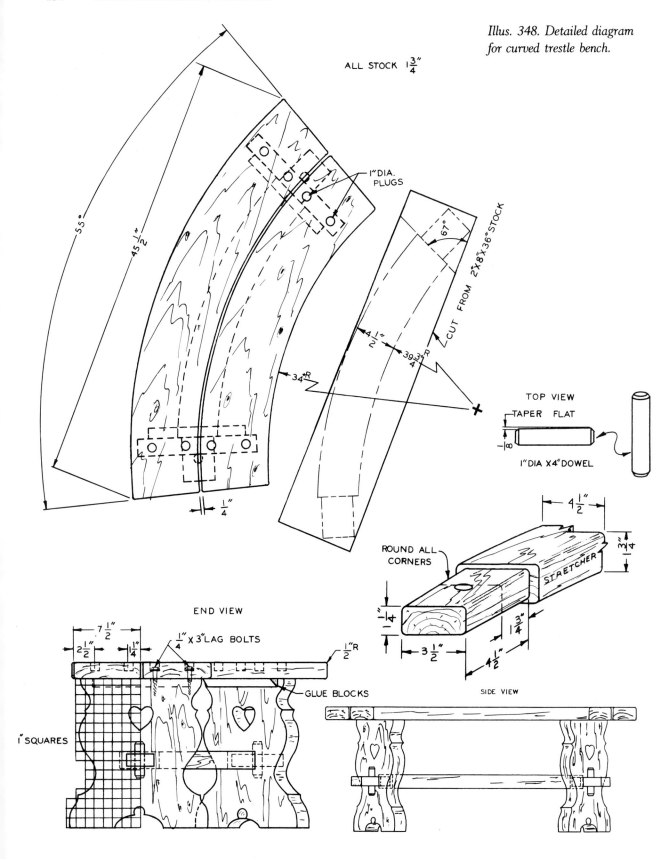

Illus. 348. Detailed diagram for curved trestle bench.

ALL STOCK 1¾"

55°

45½"

1"DIA. PLUGS

67°

CUT FROM 2"×8"×36"STOCK

4½"

39¾"R

34"R

¼"

TOP VIEW

TAPER FLAT

⅛"

1"DIA×4"DOWEL

ROUND ALL CORNERS

STRETCHER

4½"

3¾"

1¼"

3½"

1¾"

4½"

SIDE VIEW

END VIEW

7½"

2½"

¼"

¼"×3"LAG BOLTS

½"R

GLUE BLOCKS

1"SQUARES

Illus. 349. 4-foot rustic coffee
table with square edges.

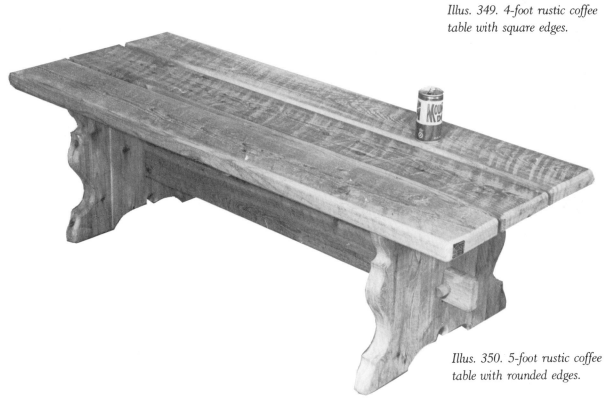

Illus. 350. 5-foot rustic coffee
table with rounded edges.

TOP VIEW

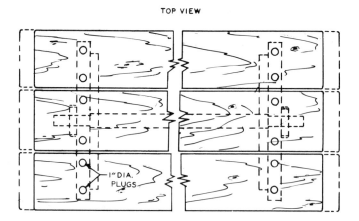

Illus. 351. Diagram for 4-foot and 5-foot coffee tables.

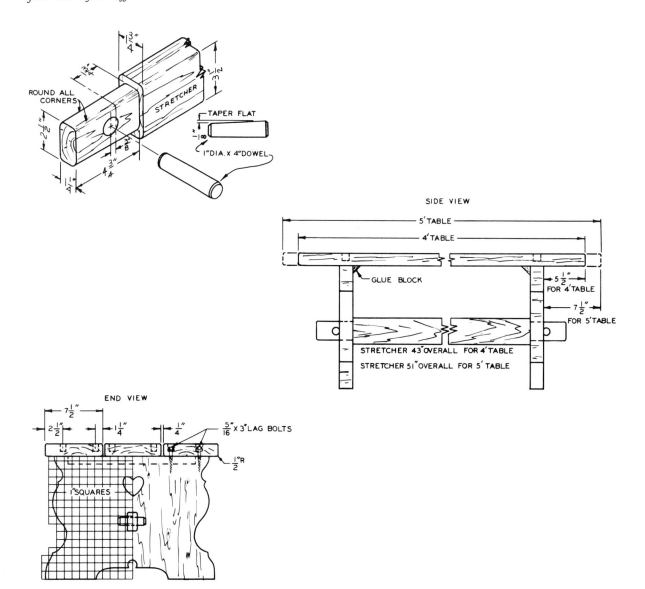

Illus. 352. 5-foot trestle table and bench set.

Illus. 353. Standard-style trestle bench with square edges.

Illus. 354. The popular 2½-foot trestle bench with heart design and rounded edges. One plan gives all details for making the trestle benches in 2½- , 3- , 4- , 5- , and 6-foot lengths. See page 159.

Illus. 355. An interesting view of our most popular picnic table set. One plan gives all picnic table details in 4- , 5- , and 6-foot sizes. See page 159.

Illus. 356. The Wood Works' 6-foot set with 2½-foot benches at each end maximizes seating capacity.

Illus. 357. Standard park bench. Naturally rustic, wayne-edged planks are combined with man-made "wear edge" rasping.

Illus. 358. Another view of similar park bench.

Illus. 359. A stylized version of the Wood Works' standard park bench. One plan gives all details for making our standard or stylized park bench in 4- and 5-foot sizes, including optional addition of arms. See page 159.

Illus. 360. Another view of the park bench design. It's doubtful if any other plan or commercially made bench affords as much comfort.

Illus. 361. One of many possible groupings.

Illus. 362. 4-foot park bench and the 5-foot size (with arms) shown with the 4-foot coffee table.

Illus. 363. The 5-foot park bench is comfortable, extremely sturdy and durable.

Illus. 364. This bench rocker includes similar construction details.

Illus. 365. The ultimate in comfort is this 5-foot bench rocker with arms. One plan gives all details for 4- and 5-foot rockers with optional arm details. See page 159.

Illus. 366. A unique design is our rocking chair. The plan is available by mail. See page 159.

Illus. 367. 4-foot swing.

Illus. 368. 5-foot swing set with arms. Ordering one plan gives all details for 4- and 5-foot swing sets with optional arms along with specific details for making the supporting A-frame structure. See page 159.

Illus. 369. S-hook link makes adjusting back tilt easy. See pages 70 and 71 for more illustrations of swing-frame construction.

Index

Numbers in italics refer to pages with illustrations.

PLANS—PRICE LIST

Notice: Spielmans Wood Works retains all rights to designs and plans. Commercial use or application in any form for profit is prohibited.

Mailbox Plan Kit. Complete, detailed plans and illustrated instructions for woodworkers to make their own rural wooden mailboxes. Special clamps not required. Includes: metallic-looking plastic for flag and straps and also plans for the standard post (page 127). $9.95 ppd.

Plans for Mailbox Post with Paper Tube (page 127). $3.50 ppd.

Plans for Arm-type Mailbox Posts. Dovetail arm, double arm for hanging signs, mortise-and-tenon, and boxed arm for paper (page 127). $4.50 ppd.

Plans for Trestle Benches. Includes plans for 2½- , 3- , 4- , 5- , and 6-foot sizes (page 153). $3.75 ppd.

Plans for Trestle Picnic Table Set. Includes all bench plans for above and plans for 4- , 5- , and 6-foot tables (page 153). $6.00 ppd.

Plans for Park Benches. Standard and stylized designs in 4- and 5-foot sizes with optional arms (page 154). $5.00 ppd.

Plans for Bench Rockers. In 4- and 5-foot sizes with optional arms (page 155). $5.00 ppd.

Plans for Rocking Chair with Arms (page 156). $3.75 ppd.

Plans for Swing Sets. In 4- and 5-foot sizes with optional arms; includes A-frame stand (page 156). $6.00 ppd.

Note: You can also order these items assembled or in knocked-down or premachined kits.

Send orders to:
Spielmans Wood Works
3771 Gibraltar Road
Fish Creek, Wisconsin 54212

CURRENT BOOKS BY PATRICK SPIELMAN

Working Green Wood with PEG. Covers every process for making beautiful, inexpensive projects from green wood without cracking, splitting, or warping. Hundreds of clear photos and drawings show every step from obtaining the raw wood through shaping, treating, and finishing your PEG-treated projects. 175 unusual project ideas. Lists supply sources. 160 pages.

Making Wood Signs. Designing, selecting woods, tools, and every process through finishing is clearly covered. Hand-carved, power-carved, routed, and sandblasted processes in small to huge signs are presented. Foolproof guides for professional letters and ornaments. Hundreds of photos (4 pages in full color). Lists sources for supplies and special tooling. 144 pages.

Making Wood Decoys. A clear step-by-step approach to the basics of decoy carving. This book is abundantly illustrated with closeup photos for designing, selecting, and obtaining woods; tools; feather detailing; painting; and finishing of decorative and working decoys. Six different professional decoy artists featured. Photo gallery (4 pages in full color) along with numerous detailed plans for various popular decoys. 160 pages.

The Basic Book of Woodworking. An introductory text with over 35 chapters to sharpen the woodworker's skills.

Generously illustrated. Over 50 easy-to-make projects with plans. More than 400 illustrations. 140 pages.

Alphabets and Designs for Wood Signs. 50 alphabet patterns, plans for many decorative designs, the latest on hand carving, routing, cutouts, and sandblasting. Pricing data. Photo gallery (4 pages in color) of wood signs by professionals from across the U.S. Over 200 illustrations. 128 pages.

Router Handbook. With nearly 600 illustrations of every conceivable bit, attachment, jig, and fixture, plus every possible operation, this definitive guide has revolutionized router applications. It begins with safety and maintenance tips, then forges ahead into all aspects of dovetailing, freehanding, advanced duplication, and more. Details for over 50 projects are included. 224 pages.

Realistic Decoys. Spielman and master carver Keith Bridenhagen reveal their successful techniques for carving, feather-texturing, painting, and finishing wood decoys. Details that you can't find elsewhere—anatomy, attitudes, markings, and the easy step-by-step approach to perfect delicate procedures—make this book invaluable. Includes listings for contests, shows, and sources of tools and supplies. 274 closeup photos, 28 in color. 224 pages.

ABOUT THE AUTHOR

Patrick Spielman's love of wood began when, as a child, he transformed fruit crates into toys. Now this prolific and innovative woodworker is respected worldwide as a teacher and author.

His most famous contribution to the woodworking field has been his perfection of a method to season green wood with polyethylene glycol 1000 (PEG). He went on to invent, manufacture, and distribute the PEG-Thermovat chemical seasoning system.

During his many years as shop instructor in Wisconsin, Spielman published manuals, teaching guides, and more than 14 popular books, including *Modern Wood Technology*, a college text. He also wrote six educational series on wood technology, tool use, processing techniques, design, and wood-product planning.

Author of the best-selling *Router Handbook* (over 110,000 copies sold), Spielman has served as editorial

consultant to a professional magazine, and his products, techniques, and many books have been featured in numerous periodicals.

This pioneer of new ideas and inventor of countless jigs, fixtures, and designs used throughout the world is a unique combination of expert woodworker and brilliant teacher—all of which endear him to his many readers and to his publisher.

At Spielmans Wood Works in the woods of northern Door County, Wisconsin, he and his family create and sell some of the most durable and popular furniture products and designs available.

Should you wish to write Pat, please forward your letters to Sterling Publishing Company.

CHARLES NURNBERG
STERLING PUBLISHING COMPANY